A FRAGILE CRAFT

SOCIETY OF BIBLICAL LITERATURE

Biblical Scholarship
in
North America

edited by
Robert W. Funk
and
Kent Harold Richards

NUMBER 3

A FRAGILE CRAFT
THE WORK OF AMOS NIVEN WILDER
John Dominic Crossan

JOHN DOMINIC CROSSAN

A FRAGILE CRAFT
The Work of
Amos Niven Wilder

BIP88

SCHOLARS PRESS

Distributed by
Scholars Press
101 Salem Street
Chico, CA 95926

A FRAGILE CRAFT
The Work of Amos Niven Wilder
John Dominic Crossan

Library of Congress Cataloging in Publication Data

Crossan John Dominic.
  A fragile craft.

  (Biblical Scholarship in North America; 3)
  Bibliography: p.
  1. Wilder, Amos Niven, 1895- I. Title. II. Series III.
Series: Biblical Scholarship in North America; 3.
BS2351.W54C76   230'.044   80-19755
ISBN 0-89130-424-X (pbk.)

Printed in the United States of America
1   2   3   4   5
Edwards Brothers, Inc.
Ann Arbor, Michigan 48106

Before and after let us not look,
but rather as in a fragile craft
be rocked on the sea.

"Autumn Fires"
(1961a:11, 1972a:31)

CONTENTS

FOREWORD
A Tribute to Amos Niven Wilder

at the occasion of his receiving *The Poetics of Faith,* a collection of essays in his honor (*Semeia*, Vols. 12 and 13), on November 20, 1978, at the Joint Annual Meeting of the American Academy of Religion and the Society of Biblical Literature in New Orleans.

> Now lasting are Faith, Hope, Love, those three—yet foremost among them is Love.

I

The hardest task for a poet is to redeem the word Love.
For it has suffered inflation in all realms of discourse—not least theological.

Love is not an overly frequent word in your writings, poems, or prose. But the sum total of your work is a redemption of Love as a mode of being, as a style of speaking, as a way of thinking.

There is the power of prophetic vision, of hope and faith open to the future, without lambasting the past or the present, without seeking scapegoats to be whipped by ridicule or sarcasm.

Your visions and hopes, your expressed hope, and hunger for things that may come—the new charts, the new maps, the new algebras—are not offered in explicit contrast to the ridiculous now or the awkward past, those negative images in which many a so-called prophet wallows, feeing utterly superior. Yours is a langauge of confession without the accompanying *anathema sit*.
Take your "New Aphrodite":

> Messiah-maid, Messiah-mother, when,
> when shalt thou bring thy gentler regimen,
> Set thy mild ban upon the sons of men
> And mollify
> Our cruelty?

A *mild* ban—to be sure, that is non-violent language, the language of love.

II

The non-violent speech, the non-violent voice, the still, small voice. It took me some time to discern the power, the awesome power of one who never felt the need to raise his voice — let alone to shout. Not even a gesture. What restraint, what faith in the authentic word, the authentic image!

And now that style, that lastingly powerful style strikes me as another sign of love — of being afraid to bruise, afraid of pulling up the wheat with the weeds.
Your way of speaking is a parable of the conditions of the power of the Kingdom before its coming in its power.
Non-violent — loving — tender.

III

Symbols die and come alive.
You are not the only one who said so. But your way of thinking about it is different.
When *you* say so, you do not paint with glee — no *Schadenfreude* (that is it: No *Schadenfreude*).
Those tumbling old symbols.
You mourn with those who feel the loss,
you point to the surprises of the old becoming new.
Your Phoenix is not that of a Hollywood show,
it is a quiet phoenix, like
the return of the migrant birds in spring time.

The bones in the valley do not rattle loud,
they just come alive in the sunshine that warms us all
lovingly, caressing.

You love not only symbols but the lovers of symbols.

IV

Therefore, as you work toward a future and a better grasp of God's gifts and mysteries, gospels and epistles, messiahs and new covenants, you have opened new vistas while remaining with us without scorn.
How alien — even wrong, or outright dumb — must much of what we say and pontificate and write seem to you.

Your poetry is part of your life,
your poetry of non-violence, the poetic incarnation of love.
That is why your work shall last, its faith, its hope
but above all its love.
Or, to put it your way, with a more humble word: Its charity.

Krister Stendahl

PREFACE

If one has learned anything from Amos Niven Wilder, it is to attend at least as much to how a writing appears as to what a writing contains. And if one has learned anything else, it is to be careful about separating such facets and thinking of them as stones laid upon stones. Those injunctions necessarily engender literary consciousness and eventually literary self-consciousness. They compel the writer to think of style as well as substance, of form as well as content, and they constrain the reader to respond not only within thematic but also within generic intentions.

Even a cursory glance at the work of Amos Niven Wilder reveals three aspects, any of which would render survey difficult. There is first of all his *breadth*. Wilder is a poet, a minister, and a scholar. His total work contains almost equal volumes of published poetry, literary criticism, and biblical commentary. An adequate analysis would have to review Wilder as a poet among poets, a literary critic among literary critics, and a biblical scholar among biblical scholars. The emphases of the present volume's series might indicate a solution which would treat poetry and criticism as refined intellectual or literary hobbies to be passed over swiftly towards a concentration on the biblical works. Such a solution is, however, quite impossible since Wilder's work is too much of a unity to allow such casual dismemberment and also because the precise power of his biblical studies lies in their genesis within such a unified and unifying vision.

Add to that, then, a second aspect, the *length* of Wilder's written career. His work, located in book-reviews and journals, essays and books, is spread over almost sixty years of publication. Arthur J. Dewey has compiled an excellent bibliography of Wilder's works to conclude *The Poetics of Faith: Essays Offered to Amos Niven Wilder* in *Semeia* 12–13 (1978). The earliest item in this bibliography is the poem, "Yale, June 1920," published in *Yale Alumni Weekly* 29/40 (1920). The latest work I know of is still in manuscript form on my desk as this preface is being written. Wilder's published works range already from 1920 to 1980.

This second aspect of length could be considered as a minor problem in volume except that it merges with the third aspect which is that of *growth*. Throughout those sixty years and whether one is concerned with poetry, criticism, or theology, one is struck by the phenomenon of Wilder's ability to continue exploring. He has never settled down on Ithaca and let age become a substitute for thought.

In approaching the work of Amos Niven Wilder, then, these were the three facets of the problem as I saw it. My solution moved along two connected lines. First, there was the question of the *genre* to be chosen. This book is not a biography, not even in the sense of an intellectual biography. Such an enterprise would have demanded far more intimate knowledge or far more intensive work than was available for its writing. I am not pleading the limitations of a short book. I am admitting that the research for such a book would have demanded far more time than I could give to it. It is, rather, an *oeuvre review,* a corpus review of the collected works of an eminent scholar. It is, therefore, book review writ large. But book review is not museum catalogue. Nobody writes reviews of books which, however magnificent they once were, are now quite dead and require from us only the pieties of an appropriate funeral and a fitting epitaph. My generic decision is, in other words, an immediate claim about the vitality and currency of the works involved.

Second, there is the even more delicate question of the *style* to be adopted. Following the mode of the book review, I wanted both to summarize as fairly as possible what Wilder was saying and also to maintain a running debate with it as we progressed. The dangers of such a procedure are obvious and they account for the paucity of good reviews around. There is an immediate objection *ad extra.* Wilder has pleaded for decades with the Society of Biblical Literature (and Exegesis) to take seriously the presence of that word Literature in its title. He has said repeatedly, and demonstrated continually, that one cannot be an adequate exegete without *both* the tools of philosophy and history *as well as* those of literature and hermeneutics. He has said this steadily but not stridently. He has been heard politely and even respectfully; but only in the seventies, with almost agonizing slowness and belatedness, are his pleadings beginning to take effect. Since he has been right for so long and alone for so long, would it not be better to insist on how essentially right and farsighted he has always been and how defective and nearsighted were those who ignored him? It could be done that way, and there would be certain gleeful pleasure in the process. It is possible in reviewing Wilder to note regularly that much of what he was saying has still not been sufficiently heard let alone debated. For example, what he has been saying for so long concerning the rhetoric of apocalyptic language or the nature of eschatological symbolism has still not penetrated into much, if any, of the work done in those areas within biblical studies. Still, it is not my intention in this book to announce Wilder's victory and to polish his weapons for reverent inclusion in some final museum. It is rather my hope that by our interchanges both our weapons may be sharpened for further use on future fields. And this brings up the second danger of the *oeuvre review* genre, which is that I might pull Wilder unfairly out of his own situation and into my own. I am very aware of this danger, and it would be much easier to avoid it if Wilder had offered some magnificent contribution in the safely distant past rather than steadily developing his own position right up to the immediate present. Once again, however, I can only hope that, even though arriving late on the scene and coming from elsewhere, I now stand sufficiently within that opening created single-handedly by Amos Niven Wilder not to betray either him or it.

After genre and style, it remains only to add a few words concerning the *structure* of this book. Those twin *Semeia* volumes already mentioned were given as *Festschrift* to Professor Wilder at the Joint Annual Meeting of the Society of Biblical Literature and the American Academy of Religion in New Orleans, 20 November 1978, and were edited by William A. Beardslee. The diversity of scholarship represented by the participants bears witness to the breadth, length, and growth of Wilder's influence. And the subtitles of the two volumes specify the breadth, length, and growth of Wilder's own literary and theological concerns. Part 1 (*Semeia* 12) is on "Rhetoric, Eschatology, and Ethics in the New Testament," and Part 2 (*Semeia* 13) considers "Imagination, Rhetoric, and the Disclosures of Faith." This rich diversity presents an organizational and presentational problem for a reviewer like myself. Had Wilder confined himself to biblical criticism, a simple chronological outline would easily have sufficed as skeletal framework for thematic emphases. It seems to me, however, that the powerful fecundity of Wilder's mind is generated by a dialectic between literature and life that appears again and again under differing titles and specifics throughout his work. It is even exemplified, I suppose, by the twin volumes of his *Semeia* celebration. I decided, therefore, to structure my *oeuvre review* so as to underline this generative dialectic as it proceeds through three deepening levels of investigation: first, eschatology and ethics; then, literature and bible; and finally, imagination and religion. And throughout the book I have kept to dialectical subtitles quite deliberately.

The poet and scholar, minister and teacher whose work is here discussed has not yet finished that work. But in that very openness and unfinishedness we have all received a most precious gift. From Amos Niven Wilder we have already learned how, gracefully as a scholar and graciously as a person, to grow old without aging.

18 September 1979

PROLOGUE
Fragility and Craft

Text

CRAFT . . . 1 *obs* : STRENGTH, FORCE . . . 2: skillfulness in plan-
ning, making or executing : artistic dexterity . . . 3 a : an occupation,
trade, or pursuit requiring manual dexterity or the application of artistic
skill . . . 4 a *obs* : EXPEDIENT, TRICK, ARTIFICE . . . : CUNNING,
GUILE . . . 5 a : the members of a particular trade or an association of
these : GUILD . . . 6 *pl usu* CRAFT a : a boat esp. of small size . . .

Webster's Third New International Dictionary

Commentary

Volume 2 of *The Works of Edgar Allen Poe,* edited by Edmund C.
Stedman and George E. Woodbury (New York: Scribner's, 1914), is
devoted to "Tales of the Grotesque and Arabesque." The second
division of these stories is composed of "Tales of Conscience, Natural
Beauty, and Pseudo-Science." Among such pseudoscientific stories there
appears a tale entitled "A Descent into the Maelström" (pp. 285–312).

The story has an epigraph from one Joseph Glanville which states
that, "The ways of God in Nature, as in Providence, are not as our
ways; nor are the models that we frame any way commensurate to the
vastness, profundity, and unsearchableness of His works, *which have a
depth in them greater than the well of Democritus.*"

"Close upon the Norwegian coast — in the sixty-eighth degree of
latitude — in the great province of Nordland — and in the dreary district
of Lofodon" (286) there was a gigantic whirlpool, a "terrific funnel,
whose interior, as far as the eye could fathom it, was a smooth, shining,
and jet-black wall of water, inclined to the horizon at an angle of some
forty-five degrees, speeding dizzily round and round with a swaying and
sweltering motion, and sending forth to the winds an appalling voice,
half shriek, half roar, such as not even the mighty cataract of Niagara
ever lifts up in its agony to Heaven" (289–90).

Three "brothers once owned a schooner-rigged smack of about
seventy tons burden, with which [they] were in the habit of fishing
among the islands" (294) at a safe distance from the great whirlpool.
One day, "the tenth of July, 18 —, a day which the people of this part of
the world will never forget," the three, caught between the islands by
"the most terrible hurricane that ever came out of the heavens" (297),
were driven inexorably towards the rim of the maelstrom.

The youngest brother immediately lashed himself to the mainmast
for safety but "both our masts went by the board as if they had been

sawed off" (298) and he was drowned before the boat even reached the whirlpool's outermost pull.

The eldest brother clung desperately to a ring-bolt near the foot of the foremast as the boat was swept over the rim of the vortex and whirled around "as if by magic, midway down, upon the interior surface of a funnel vast in circumference, prodigious in depth, and whose perfectly smooth sides might have been mistaken for ebony, but for the bewildering rapidity with which they spun around, and for the gleaming and ghastly radiance they shot forth, as the rays of the full moon, from that circular rift amid the clouds . . . streamed in a flood of golden glory along the black walls, and far away down into the inmost recesses of the abyss" (306). Despite signals from his brother, he "refused to move from his station by the ring-bolt," and he was hurtled downwards as the boat "made three or four wild gyrations in rapid succession, and . . . plunged headlong, at once and forever, into the chaos of foam below" (311).

The middle brother noticed that heavier objects, such as their boat, were being whirled down into the depths with ever increasing speed while lighter objects were being whirled upwards towards the rim rather than downwards towards the abyss. He immediately "resolved to lash myself securely to the water cask upon which I now held, to cut it loose from the counter, and to throw myself with it into the water" (310). As he expected, the cask was eventually spun up and over the rim of the whirlpool, where, as he concludes his story, "a boat picked me up— exhausted from fatigue—and (now that the danger was removed) speechless from the memory of its horror. Those who drew me on board were my old mates and daily companions, but they knew me no more than they would have known a traveller from the spirit-land. My hair, which had been raven-black the day before, was as white as you see it now. They say too that the whole expression of my countenance had changed. I told them my story—they did not believe it. I now tell it to you—and I can scarcely expect you to put more faith in it than did the merry fishermen of Lofoden" (312).

CHAPTER 1
ESCHATOLOGY AND ETHICS

On one occasion I stopped my Model T Ford ambulance by the road, where several [French soldiers] were having their noonday meal. They welcomed me into their animated argot and sliced off for me portions of their army bread and sausage. The American late comer in his smart whipcord uniform from Lloyd's felt that he was initiated into a faded horizon-blue fraternity which stretched from the Jura and the Vosges to Verdun and the Somme, into a solidarity that extended back three years, and even further to the times of Napoleon and Joan of Arc. History should have a place for these kinds of nuances and diapasons.

(1975a:115)

There are veiled powers that live our lives; there are arcane transactions beneath the surface of experience that made fate for us; there are buried hierophanies and scenarios which are still potent in our orientation to existence . . .
One such archaic motif is that of spiritual Armageddon, or war in heaven, involving the living. To give a concrete example I cite my own transcription of a World War I experience in which the actual duress took on mythical extrapolation.

There we marched out on haunted battle-ground,
There smelled the strife of gods, were brushed against
By higher beings, and were wrapped around
With passions not of earth, all dimly sensed.

(1971a:436–37)

1.1   War and Eschaton

Amos Wilder's interest in eschatology spans forty years of scholarly publications, from "The Nature of Jewish Eschatology" in 1931 to "The Rhetoric of Ancient and Modern Apocalyptic" in 1971a. The origins of that interest go back at least as far as his classes at Oxford University in 1921–23. Besides such teachers as C.H. Dodd and B.H. Streeter, there was also an association with Albert Schweitzer. Forty years later Amos Wilder wrote in remembrance: "In 1922, I was a student at Mansfield College, where Schweitzer was giving the Dale Lectures in French, part of his later *Philosophy of Civilization*. Because of my knowledge of French I had the opportunity of aiding him in slight ways with his correspondence and appointments. These contacts combined with the reading of *The Quest of the Historical Jesus,* led to my life-long interest in New Testament eschatology, but also to a more significant understanding of the gospel and the Christian life" (1962a:361–62). And in another recollection, almost sixty years after the event, he added further details.

"At that period Schweitzer was raising money by his organ concerts to restore his hospital and further his work at Lambarene after his enforced absence during WW I. Since I knew French I served as a kind of amanuensis to him with his correspondence. The Schweitzers had a room in the home of the College Principal, Dr. Selbie. The great doctor worked incessantly at irregular hours. He was a massive figure, and Mrs. Selbie plaintively admitted that even his step or a clearing of his throat at 3 A.M. could shake the house!" (1980).

But Wilder's interest in eschatology may go back even earlier, to 1918 and a different form of education when,

> . . . one summer night
> We toiled obscurely through a mighty wood
> Teeming with desperate armies; toiled to smite
> At dawn upon the unsuspecting height
> Above, the Powers of Darkness, where they stood . . .

The introduction to that poem, "Armageddon" (1928:45), notes that,

> The crux and turning-point of the World War is usually assigned to the dawn of July 18, 1918. At that time, after a feverish mobilization in the great woods near Soissons of Highlander, Moroccan, and other units, including the first and second American divisions, General Mangin, under Marshal Foch's orders, attacked eastward, threatening the German Marne salient. The desperate rush to the front in the great beech forests during that rainy night and the attack at 4:25 remain one of the outstanding epic actions of the war. The overtones of the event and its portentous significance were obscurely felt by those who took part in it.

Thus, even if only "obscurely felt" or "dimly sensed" (1923:31) or "obscurely recognized . . . we construed the apocalyptic overtones of the war and of such actions as the attack at dawn on July 18, 1918, in the forest of Villers-Cotterêts or that of November 1 in the Argonne" (1968a:355). Wilder himself had gone as a volunteer "to France in the fall of 1916. After a winter with the Paris section he joined Section 2 of the American Field Service in February, 1917, and then Section 3 in Serbia in July. When the United States Army took over the ambulance sections, he enlisted in Paris in the United States Field Artillery in November, 1917. He served as a corporal in [A Battery of] the 17th Field Artillery of the 2nd [Indian Head] Division and was discharged in France in June, 1919" (1968a:344, my additions). Eschatological Armageddon, so imminently future for many biblical seers, began for Wilder as "battle retrospect" (1923:7–10). Much later, however, when "after 50 years I thought it was time to attend at least one national reunion of my World War I battery and division . . . in Des Moines . . . I rudely realized that my opinions found little echo—whether about ethnic issues, welfare policies, campus disturbances, ROTC or Viet Nam" (1974a:104). Even a shared eschatology could not guarantee a shared ethics.

By the time that poem, "Armageddon," appeared in his second book of poems (1928:45–49), Wilder had just completed three years as a Congregational minister in North Conway, New Hampshire. A marriage performed during that ministry became the poem "Marriage of Minors" (1932:735, 1943a:73–74), and he has cited this poem to exemplify how "my poetry was always for me a kind of precipitate of experience, cherished rather as record than as art-work" (1978b:34).

Wilder then returned to graduate study at Yale and Harvard (1928–1930), and thence became Associate Professor of Ethics and Christian Evidences at Hamilton College in Clinton, New York (1930–1933). His dissertation, through summers spent in the Yale library, was completed in 1933, and he then became Norris Professor of New Testament at Andover Newton Theological School (1933–1943).

The title of his dissertation is, as demanded by the protocols of that genre, quite precise: *The Relation of Eschatology to Ethics in the Teaching of Jesus as Represented in Matthew* (1933). From that conjunction one could have moved in any of four distinct directions: (1) Matthew, (2) Jesus, (3) Ethics, (4) Eschatology. Wilder's choice among these options and his progress along the chosen lines have been quite definite and deliberate.

1.2   Jesus and Eschaton

Wilder's dissertation could have led him to an interest in the evangelist Matthew, towards what we now term redactional or compositional criticism. It did not do so. Twenty years later, the seventh volume of *The Interpreter's Bible* contained a section on "The Sermon on the Mount" by Wilder (1951a:155–64), but it was under the division on "The Teaching of Jesus" and not under the following one on "The Gospel according to St. Matthew." Had he gone towards Matthew, towards a critical appraisal of style and substance, form and content, medium and message in this gospel taken as a unified authorial production, one can only speculate if we would have seen "our present attempts to read a Gospel, as it stands, as the work of an author and not of a mere compiler" (1971b:143) done long before its time. It is fairly certain, at least, that Wilder would not have been so misled by the glaring form critical mistake of assuming the evangelists were collectors of units rather than creators of wholes. The first author cited in his dissertation is B.W. Bacon (1933:ii) and, in discussing "my old teacher Benjamin W. Bacon" many years later, he noted that "his early and important work on the stages of the tradition, and on the final work of the evangelists, Matthew and John, in their own right and situation—

and in primary relation to patristic and proto-gnostic contexts—all this took shape for him apart from acquaintance with the form critical pioneers. The point of this observation is not to disparage the form critics but to suggest that our understanding of the Gospels in their composition as wholes may well be served by other strategies" (1971b: 139).

Be that as it may, Wilder's primary interest in this subject then and thereafter was not with the authorial Matthew but with the historical Jesus. And here an ambiguity must be noted which has been characteristic not only of his own work but of most modern biblical research on this point.

The roots of this ambiguity may be traced back to those who advised and consented on the dissertation itself. Writing much later, Wilder has recalled the situation in 1929 (1980):

> The committee for my projected dissertation on eschatology and ethics in the teaching of Jesus included Kraeling, Campbell and Erwin Goodenough. Since I had completed residence requirements at Yale it was agreed that I could well get the benefit of study at Harvard and especially suggestions from Kirsopp Lake in the further defining of my topic. Anyone working in the line of Schweitzer was at this time under some handicaps. I have under my eye as I write a letter from Walter Lowrie in September of 1929 just as I was settling in to Divinity Hall at Cambridge . . . Lowrie wrote:
>> For myself I have serious counsel to give you. If you would have long life and would see good days, keep mum on the subject of eschatology. It will be better if you do not read my book . . . [*Jesus According to St. Mark* (1929)]. I am afraid our conversations at Babbio may reillumine your interest in a subject which is highly dangerous in these days. Your teachers give you good advice: eschatology is a subject which the good and the great conspire to shun.
> I had an interview with Kirsopp Lake and A.D. Nock the day after my arrival at Harvard and the upshot rather tended to confirm Lowrie's forebodings. Lake observed that I could deal with Jesus's eschatology but that I would just come out with another theory about it. One could discuss the data but there were not enough data to reach a conclusion. But then he listed certain problems that merited discussion, such as the relation of the Church to eschatological salvation . . . Lake later wisely steered me into limiting myself to the Gospel of Matthew, but within this encompass I was encouraged to go on with my study of eschatology and ethics.

The problem can be specified by indicating three successive stages in the Preface of Wilder's dissertation. In the first stage he stresses the gulf that yawns between the historical Jesus and the authorial Matthew. There is a series of negative statements concerning our knowledge of the former followed by positive ones concerning the latter. Of the historical Jesus he says (1933:iii–v):

But the task of finding out what the original teaching of Jesus himself was either as regards eschatology or ethics is so beset with difficulties that an investigation at these points could not lead us to any solidly accredited results. This same holds as regards any study of the relationship of eschatology to ethics in the teaching of Jesus himself. The only hope would be that the topic could be sketched and a working hypothesis offered . . . The actual words of Jesus, and, another question, his actual views (which may not be at all fully represented in what actual words we could assign him) are so subject to dispute that we may well refuse to try to build upon a selection however made . . . We recognize that each gospel has diverse strata. This fact will add difficulty to any effort to bring into a single focus the teaching of Jesus upon any given topic. Indeed, buried in these strata lies that one representing the original teaching of Jesus himself at least in partial record, a stratum certainly stranger to the modifications later transmission has imposed upon it. That, however, we cannot definitely enough isolate, nor the later increments to it or distortions of it.

These negative statements on our knowledge of the historical Jesus are now counter-pointed almost one for one by positive statements concerning the authorial Matthew (1933:iv–v):

We have here, in any case, fixed and given data for study. We are not continually thrown back on passages whose genuineness is in doubt . . . Taking one or other of the Synoptic Gospels . . . we yet have an abundance of dependable data for studying the topic as here found: the relation of eschatology to ethics in the teaching of Jesus *as represented to us* in the particular gospel. What divergence it will give us from the situation of the historical Jesus will be more than compensated by the knowledge that we have at least something built solidly upon documents . . . Yet the book as it stands is a unit coming from one hand at a given time . . . Our first task is to see our problem as it looked to the evangelist.

These contrapuntal statements constitute a first stage of the problem. The second stage concludes, quite logically and necessarily, that in the dissertation "the Jesus we are concerned with and the Jesus repeatedly referred to is the Jesus of Mt. . . . the present study has in mind the Jesus presented in this gospel" (1933:v–vi). But then comes a third stage in which those first two stages are somehow retracted (1933:vii):

It should be emphasized, perhaps, that in surrendering the attempt to get back to the actual teaching and position of Jesus in this matter, and in confining ourselves to the problem as given us in the text of Mt., we are not really relinquishing so much as appears . . . The expectation of an imminent Judgment seems to have been constant from the preaching of John through that of Jesus and through the early period of the church. Again, the ethical precepts of Jesus were not essentially modified over the period between his teaching and that of the writing of the gospels.

There is thus an acute ambivalence between the historical Jesus who cannot be known, in stage one, and the historical Jesus who is essentially the same as that found in the gospels, in stage three. And I would repeat that this ambivalence is not exclusive to Wilder but is almost characteristic of the attempt of contemporary scholarship to have its daily bread and eat it too. The problem arises from the attempt, or lack of attempt, to explain both the discontinuities and the continuities between the historical Jesus, the primitive traditions, and the evangelical authors. It may well be that Wilder's last cited statements are quite correct, but they can hardly be taken for granted in the light of his former ones. If change, continual and even significant change, seems to characterize the transmission of the Jesus material, why was so much change necessary if everyone was offering essentially the same message? And, if one answers that the changes were of little significance, then why are scholars making so much of them in the first place? One is, in any case, quite dissatisfied with the intellectual integrity of scholarship's claims that: (1) we do not know the message of Jesus, but (2) we do know the messages of the evangelists, and (3) these messages are essentially the same.

Wilder returned more formally to the problem of the historical Jesus on some later occasions. The first of these is still moving within the restricted focus of his dissertational interests but others open up wider horizons.

The dissertation was published in 1939 with the abbreviated title, *Eschatology and Ethics in the Teaching of Jesus*, and this was republished in an expanded and revised version in 1950. This volume's endurance has been demonstrated not only by the sections of it incorporated into a college text-book on *The Judeo-Christian Heritage* (1970a:200–207) but also by its recent reprinting (1978a). The emphasis of the revised 1950 version has clearly shifted from the Jesus of Matthew to the Jesus of history. Not only has *as Represented in Matthew* been dropped from the title but the initial section of the dissertation on "The Eschatological Teaching of Jesus as Represented by Matthew" (1933:21–61) has been replaced by two chapters on "The Eschatological Teaching of Jesus" and "Historical and Transcendental Elements in Jesus' View of the Future" (1978a:37–70). These new chapters both expand the original dissertation and also include revised and extended versions of two articles already published by Wilder (1937a, 1948a).

The shift from authorial Matthew to historical Jesus shows up immediately as the Preface of 1933 is rewritten for 1950 (1978a) but once again a trilogy of assertions serves to continue in another format the ambivalence noted earlier for a different trilogy.

The first stage is now much more positive concerning our knowledge of the historical Jesus. Compare my first quotation given above (1933:iii) with its 1950 replacement (1978a:11–12):

The task of stating what the original teaching of Jesus himself was, either as regards eschatology or ethics, not to mention their mutual relation, is one beset with immense obstacles . . . In any case an effort must be made and has been made with good results to distinguish some of the clearer modifications which the tradition has undergone, by the use of all the criteria open to us. On the basis of these a working hypothesis as to the historical Jesus and his teaching can be presented. Such a hypothesis must underlie a study of this kind. While the detailed argument of this hypothesis is not included in the present form of this inquiry, its main points will appear.

And since knowledge of the historical Jesus has become much more positive, the contrapuntal emphases on the evangelists in general and on Matthew in particular are now removed. The second stage, then, has nothing about any focus on the Jesus of Matthew and instead it asserts that, "even supposing we err in some degree in confusing the Jesus of the gospels with the Jesus of history," this is not a serious problem. The reason is "our firm conviction that at bottom, in its essential meaning, the relation of eschatology to ethics was much the same for this community as it was for Jesus himself. The distortion has effected not the essence of the matter but the externals" (1978a:12).

But, now, once again, a third stage is presented in order to have it both ways. Earlier his third stage had asserted that there was no *historical* problem since the message of Jesus and of the church were the same. Now, a third stage claims that there is no *theological* problem, "even supposing that our best hypothesis only presents us with a Jesus created by the tradition." The reason for this is given in a quotation from Bultmann's 1929 book *Jesus* which concludes that, "'Instead of the message of Jesus, it would be the message of the community that needed exposition, and since it finally comes down to the substance, meaning and claim of the evangelical tradition, the question as to how much the historical Jesus and how much others contributed thereto would be a secondary matter'" (1978a:12–13). Once again, it would seem, we have a trilogy of assertions which is extremely ambivalent: (1) we do know the message of Jesus, but (2) even if we confuse it with the message of the evangelists, (3) it is this latter that is important in any case. Wilder has moved, with most of historical Jesus research, from saying that isolation of historical Jesus from authorial evangelists was historically impossible but also historically unnecessary in 1933 to saying that it was historically possible but also theologically inappropriate in 1950 (1978a).

In order to dissipate this ambivalence, in 1933 or in 1950, Wilder might have isolated from all the evangelical sources the complete corpus of Jesus materials that *he* judged to be historically original, and then might have studied this separated corpus in both its style and substance, form and content, and, finally, some valid comparison might have been made with the gospel visions of Jesus as well as valid decisions made on continuities and discontinuities, agreements and disagreements. He did not choose to do so, and we shall have to return to this decision again later on.

But, instead of establishing his own corpus, he opted, in his chapter on "The Eschatological Teaching of Jesus" (1948a, 1978a:37–52), for a critical review of recent studies on that subject. He began with Albert Schweitzer's interpretation of Jesus' interim ethics, imminent expectations, and eventual attempt to precipitate the eschaton (1978a:37–39). But after a survey of major European and American scholarship since Schweitzer, Wilder concludes that "the simple thorough-going eschatology of Schweitzer had been modified at some points. There is a present aspect of the Kingdom as well as the future aspect. Jesus did not teach an interim ethic in Schweitzer's sense, but in this area often spoke as though the world were to continue. Much of the apocalyptic assigned to Jesus by the Gospels is today viewed as secondary" (1978a:50). Finally, he concludes with his own understanding of Jesus' eschatology. Wilder maintains that Jesus "saw a world-process under way and moving toward its climax . . . the arriving eschaton. Its outcome he saw as the Kingdom of God or the life of the age to come" (1978a:51). This, however, is only one aspect of it because Jesus "could speak of the future in less dualistic fashion . . . could envisage the future in non-dualistic, non-apocalyptic terms" (1978a:51). Thus Wilder agrees with Rudolf Otto that "the intentionality of the eschatological type was manifest in him: he could announce the imminent end of the world but live and teach as if it were to go on" (1978a:52).

It is clear that even scholars who share an identical *corpus* or database of material can disagree quite fundamentally on the *commentary*. But it is even clearer that, if there is no such agreement on *corpus*, one must discuss this before proceeding on to *commentary*. In reviewing scholarly options up to 1950 and in attempting to base himself on a critical position within it, Wilder is dealing with commentators who may disagree quite completely on the corpus of Jesus materials each takes to be historically original. They include and discuss certain ones, of course, but one seldom knows all the others which are excluded. This is true up to 1950, and it is also true of some subsequent articles (1963) and book reviews (1964c) Wilder wrote on the same subject at later dates.

In 1963 Wilder wrote the only article he formally devoted to this problem, "The New Quest for the Historical Jesus." Once again there is little discussion of corpus; but continuity is affirmed by stating that "This constant may be defined in terms of the radical eschatological consciousness of both Jesus and his post-Easter followers, including both its joy and its claims. *We do not mean here common ideas or terminology.* For both Jesus and the church the meaning of life was determined by the presence of a world-renewal paralleling that of the creation itself and seen first of all as grace. It was not long before the church was actually portraying this renewal in cosmological terms. *Jesus and the first Christians used Jewish-apocalyptic terms"* (1963:247). I have italicized words whose simultaneous assertion seems problematic to me but, for the moment, I prefer to emphasize a different point. Since Wilder is talking, in this article, mostly of Ernst Fuchs and his understanding of parable as *Sprachereignis*, he exemplifies from the parable of The Sower. One suddenly realizes how little attention Wilder has paid to the parables of Jesus despite the expectation that his literary sensitivity might have drawn him very early to their consideration. They are discussed, of course, along with other modes and genres of early Christian rhetoric (1971b), and Wilder knows that in the parables "we have the one element in the Gospels of any extent which after due sifting we can hold as original with little question" (1971b:87). Yet it would be another ten years before he devoted a study to a specific parable and that, once again, was the parable of The Sower (1974b).

When that last point is placed alongside the main one I have been making in this section, namely, that Wilder never attempts to establish the limits of the corpus of Jesus materials he accepts as original, one conclusion becomes clear. Wilder did not move from his dissertation in the direction of the authorial Matthew as a focus of interest and neither, nor, in the long run, did he move towards the historical Jesus. Even if Jesus received much more later attention than did Matthew, the focus would always remain on the first half of his dissertation's title, on eschatology and ethics, and on the former primarily because of the latter, on eschatology because of ethics rather than on ethics because of eschatology.

1.3   Ethic and Eschaton

The emphasis here is on ethics rather than on eschatology since I shall have to return to eschatology again in the next section.

The opening chapter of Wilder's dissertation was on "The Nature and Ethical Aspects of Jewish Eschatology" (1933:1–20) which expanded an article on the same subject published in 1931. I shall summarize his position by a series of key statements:

> Eschatology is myth. But whereas most myth represents the unknown past and gives a symbolic picture of unknown origins, eschatology is that form of myth which represents the unknown future. (1931:1)

> The world's greatest myths have always been summary and symbolic representations of essential truths. (1933:3)

> The imminence of the eschatological event is a particular problem. In general it seems to be in proportion to the intensity of faith. (1933:4)

Faith under certain circumstances, discouraging circumstances, looks to the compensations of God. Oppression, times of extreme effort, martyrdom, the sway of evil, these demand a divine reversal provided the sense of divine actuality and holiness is sufficiently alive. (1933:6)

Ethics was inextricably implied in the best apocalyptic. It was presumed. The eschatological hope was only for those who were righteous. And it was the ethical consciousness which in the first place demanded the Kingdom. (1933:15)

Behind that series of quotations there is one major problem concerning the *symbolic/literal* distinction in the intention and interpretation of eschatological imagery. Wilder devotes much more space to this than I have indicated by my citations (1933:7–12). He contends, on the one hand, that "it is probable that we lend a false concreteness to their anticipations. It is a very real problem here to know just what they really expected when they used apocalyptic imagery . . . On the one hand we take them too literally and ignore the poetical mentality of the race and the age. On the other hand we make a mistake if we think of them as merely symbol and poetry as a modern would understand them" (1933:7). And again, later, he claims that "we may say that the Jewish eschatological program was 'symbolic' only, provided we bear in mind that the distinction of historical and imaginative was not clear cut to them" (1933:8). On the other hand, Wilder also admits that "the visions at first and in their later creative examples were imaginative in intention. But in varying measure they were taken realistically and imitated realistically" (1933:11). But if it is plausibly possible to introduce "a crass literalness of understanding" (1933:10), so that "the common Christian and Jewish imagination has literalized eschatology" (1933:11–12), there must be something present in eschatological symbolism that allowed such developments, or maybe even provoked and insured them. Whether one is impressed or not by appeals to the naive mind of primitive poetics, and I am emphatically not, there is still a problem where symbolic intention begets literal interpretation with such speed and regularity. There is no problem with symbolic myths of ending; and, indeed, one expects them after finding symbolic myths of beginning. But, as Wilder himself specifies, "imminence . . . is a particular problem" (1933:4) and it is an especial problem when it is linked, as here, with persecution and martyrdom. I am inclined to formulate a hypothetical rule and assert that the more present the persecution, the more literal the imminence of its vindication. Is "the imminence . . . in proportion to the intensity of the faith" as Wilder suggests (1933:4) or is the imminence in proportion to the intensity of the pain? Again: do those who need the message most desperately read it most literally, while those who need it with less physical or mental desperation hear it with more symbolic interpretation? Granted that an interplay of univalence and polyvalence is present in all symbolism, does eschatological symbolism exploit this in some very special way? Does the brilliance of the imagery, combined with the fragmentation of its narrative syntax inevitably produce both the most ethereal transcendentalism and the most crass literalism? Could it even be said that the world-loss and language-loss which confronts the eschatological imagination with the impossible challenge of projecting hope beyond hopelessness and meaning beyond meaninglessness must operate at a level prior to any such distinction as literal and symbolic?

I will let these questions hold for the moment since Wilder returns to them in later studies. But it must be noted that the more one insists on the symbolism of eschatology, the more difficulty one will have in establishing the literalism of the ethics derived from it or based on it.

In the dissertation context of the Matthean Jesus, eschatology is discussed in terms of the *sanction* (1933: 62–152) and the *content* ("differentia") of the ethics (1933:153–224) and these twin subjects form the core of the revised 1950 book based on it (1978a:71–141, 143–183). Wilder's conclusion has remained exactly the same from dissertation through publication and revision (1933:225 = 1978a:187).

> The sanction of the ethics arises from the anticipation of the culminating features of those times, the Judgment. But that Judgment is only a formal sanction; the conceptions of the parousia and the subsequent retributions and the regeneration are essentially imaginative. Therefore they do not require and involve an interim-ethic, and such we see, indeed, to be the case. For the ethics in themselves ignore an imminent catastrophe. Their true sanction evidently is something else: whatever lies behind the symbolic picture of Judgment. This something else, the true sanction, is the fact of God and his nature and his will with men as assented to by the discernment of mind and heart. But it is this same fact which really determines the differentia of the ethics. It is the new apprehension of God and his will which compels a new ethics. In this respect the cogency of the ethics lies in their nature. In the other aspect, that of sanction, the cogency of the ethics lies in the instant perception of consequences involved in choice and in conduct where such a God is concerned.

The discussion of ethics in his dissertation had been quite limited by its focus on the Matthean Jesus and on the relationship between eschatology and ethics. Wilder's own interest in ethics went quite beyond such limitations and this was already evident in the final chapter which he added to the dissertation for its revised publication in 1950. This concerned "The Kingdom of God and the Moral Life" (1978a: 194–214) which expanded an article published some time before (1941a).

The question here is "whether there may not be a true sense in which the Kingdom of God is above good and evil and in which it transcends moral preoccupation" (1978a:195). This question involves a "consideration of the category of mysticism rather than of eschatology in examining the religious context of the ethic of the gospel" (1978a: 195); or, in other words, it involves "an eschatological mysticism in the message of Jesus resting on the sense of the glory of God and reflected in the endowment of Jesus' person" (1978a:196). This eschatological mysticism must protect against two transformations. On the one hand, "it should not be transformed into a moralism;" but, on the other, neither should it succumb to "the risk of antinomianism" (1978a:196). At this point Wilder has universalized the problem of eschatological ethics and he concludes that "one of the chief services that biblical theology can render today is to show how moralism can be avoided without a lapse into ethical irresponsibility" (1978a:196). Examples of his own attempts to walk this narrow middle way appeared in articles published in the forties. He argued against moralism, in the form of absolute pacifism, that "it rises out of assumptions that lack biblical support or that apply New Testament insights beyond their relevant application" (1942a:140). And he argued against antinomianism that "it is, indeed, rhetorically impressive to say that the claims of the Kingdom 'confound' all human standards, 'dissolve' all existing patterns . . . But such excessive categories and paradoxes are better suited to the preacher than to the historian or the psychologist." Hence, "it is because the soul of man is *naturaliter Christianum* that his natural law prepares him for the ethic of the Kingdom" (1946a: 135). It is surely possible cordially to dislike both moralism and antinomianism and still not be satisfied completely with those formulations of how and why they must be opposed in the name of the eschatological mysticism of Jesus.

In 1943 Wilder moved to the Chicago Theological Seminary on the Federated Theological Faculty of the University of Chicago, and his book reviews appeared in every volume of the *Chicago Theological Seminary Register* with unfailing regularity from 1943 through 1953. An influence from the Chicago tradition of sociological emphasis entered his development in this period. Problems in eschatological ethics are now considered, for both first and twentieth centuries, in their social and political aspects. For example, towards the end of his time in Chicago, Wilder compared European and American biblical scholarship in terms of a "persistent inclination on the part of our biblical scholarship to find a this-age significance in the NT eschatology and therewith the justification for a substantial social ethic. This tendency goes back to the earlier scholars identified with the social gospel, including Orello Cone and Nathaniel Schmidt; but it is also illustrated by the later so-called Chicago School of which Shirley Jackson Case was the foremost figure,

a school which still has numerous influential representatives"
(1954a:25).

The move to Harvard Divinity School in 1954, and the appointment
as Hollis Professor of Divinity in 1955 (Emeritus since 1963), probably
had less influence on Wilder's continuing sociological emphasis than had
his participation from mid-fifties to mid-sixties on the editorial board of
Christianity and Crisis and also on various committees and projects of
the World Council of Churches.

The socio-political implications of first-century eschatology for twentieth-century society were the subject of two important articles in the
fifties (1956b, 1958a), where the phrases "kerygmatic social ethic"
(1956b:516) and "kerygmatic ethic" (1958a:137) begin to be used.

His claim here is that "the gains of New Testament study in our
time have placed in our hands a liberating principle of Biblical interpretation, namely the *kerygma*, which affords us a direct encounter with the
divine imperative, unadulterated with cultural distortions" (1956b:517).
Such an encounter must not, however, "confine the saving work of
God to the personal and individual sphere" and he considers that
"Rudolf Bultmann's understanding of the *kerygma* . . . [has] this individualistic character" (1956b:519). His own contribution is now derived from the mythical and eschatological language of Paul rather than
of Jesus. And the heart of the matter is "Paul's view of the conflict
between God or Christ or the Church and the 'principalities and
powers', the 'rulers of the world'. We have here in Paul a mythological
understanding of the victory of the Gospel over the tyrants of this
world, its false authorities" (1956b:527). This means that "Paul sees the
life of the Church and the believer, and the role of the Holy Spirit, in
terms of this dynamic and victorious struggle with social-metaphysical,
that is, cultural tyrants" so that "it is not enough to effect this
translation in individualistic, pietistic or existentialist terms. What is
represented in a naive uncritical first-century mythology must be carried
over into our thought-world in terms of a realistic Christian sociology"
(1956b:532).

The second article repeats in summary form much of the above
argument but it precedes it with one new emphasis. This consists in
placing alongside the other article's emphasis on *kerygma* an equal
emphasis on *didache*. This is necessary because "*didache* accompanies
kerygma from the beginning. Indeed, we find the same thing in the Old
Testament; a covenant of grace is always accompanied by a table of ob-
ligations" (1958a: 140). What Wilder wishes to avoid here is the idea
that *kerygma* is primary and causative while *didache* is secondary and
derivative. He contends that "what is basic to the early community is
not even the *kerygma,* but what lies behind it as divine operation and
this divine operation is not really described when we identify certain
striking events such as the works, words, death, and resurrection of

Christ. Divine action has a social character and includes these; it includes both Christ and the response to him. The divine action is seen in the creation of the community and its pattern and interrelations" (1958a:141–42). The conclusion from this is that "Christian ethics is not an 'application' of the 'Good News.' The ethics is already there in the creative divine action re-shaping human community. The new human pattern and relationships are what is *given* and not an implication of what is given" (1958a:142).

Finally, in a specifically Chicago context, he returned once again to these "Social Factors in Early Christian Eschatology" (1961b). His conclusion is that "the eschatological mood represents a radical spiritual and cultural effort of a group (or an individual) to overcome disorder and to define *meaning,* and to give body to possibilities and to the future, as well as to come to terms with dynamic and radical changes in the conditions of existence. The background for this in the centuries before and after Christ was the loss of *meaning* and relationship of many groups, whether in Jewish or pagan life" (1961b:76). Wilder has placed the emphasis on loss and gain of meaning (my italics) and therefore considers that "such elements as poverty, slavery, class or social frustration, persecution, were only elements in the more general crisis" (1961b:76).

That last article concludes a line of development from the eschatological language of the Matthean Jesus to the eschatological language of the apostle Paul and from the mythological language of the first century presentation to the socio-political language of a twentieth-century interpretation. In the process, eschatology did not *become* socio-political. It was symbolically so from the very beginning.

1.4   Rhetoric and Eschaton

The dialectic of eschatology and ethics, of eschatological language and ethical life, has been present in Wilder's work from the very first two sentences of the "Summary of Results" which prefaced his 1933 Yale dissertation: "Jewish and early Christian eschatology were essentially *symbolic* and can best be understood by the analogy of myth. They were also *ethically* inspired in the main" (1933, second unnumbered page, my italics). Symbolic and ethical, in conjunction, but in that order. One cannot then bypass the symbolic mode in any rush to the ethical imperative.

In the preceding section the emphasis was more on the ethical pole of the dialectic. But with his Presidential Address to the annual meeting of the Society of Biblical Literature and Exegesis on December 25, 1955, at Union Theological Seminary in New York, Wilder started a series of studies with greater emphasis on the "imagery" (1958b), and especially on the "rhetoric" (1956a, 1971a) of apocalyptic eschatology.

In his SBL Presidential Address, Wilder proposed that the most promising aspect "of the continuing discussion of NT mythology is what we may call the basic semantic question, rather than its theological corollaries. What is the nature of imaginative symbol?" (1956a:2). He argues that biblical scholars have to be "first of all, and rightly, philologists and historians" (1956a:2) but that, precisely as such, they find that their "tools for dealing with the symbolic elements in our texts are not altogether adequate" (1956a:8). He points to three faulty readings of symbolic or mythical texts from either a too *literal* or a too *ornamental* or a too *rational* viewpoint (1956a:2, 9). And over against this triple failure, he proposes, from the work of literary rather than historical critics, a triple emphasis to initiate an adequate approach to biblical symbolism. Mytho-poetic statements are *dynamic*, representing the "'available past' in potent form . . . for group life"; they are *untranslatable*, they "cannot be paraphrased . . . into a discursive equivalent"; and they are *polyvalent*, they represent "a fusion in one act of imagination of many contributory and often apparently contradictory aspects of experience" (1956a:9–10). Summing up his presentation, Wilder concludes that "we are dealing with a mytho-poetic mentality and not with a prosaic or discursive one. We cannot apply to the imaginative representations in question our modern alternatives of literal versus symbolic. They were meant neither literally nor symbolically, but naively" (1956a:11). One can agree with everything Wilder said up to that conclusion and still feel uneasy about its distinctions. What is this double distinction of a mytho-poetic mentality which is opposed to a prosaic or discursive one? What is this triple distinction of literal, symbolic, and naive? And what does his use of "modern" contribute to these distinctions? Above all, are we talking about evolutionary types of mind or archeological levels of mind? It is already clear that much more sophisticated grounding in linguistic theory will be needed if these distinctions are to be adequately articulated.

A few years later Wilder returned to this subject. But he did not attempt to ground the problem any more fundamentally than before. He is still talking of a "mythical mentality" or a "mythic mentality" (1958b: 230) just as earlier of a "mytho-poetic mentality" (1956a:11). His immediate purpose, however, was to specify more fully the sociological dynamism of mythical language, that is, to focus more precisely on the first of the three aspects of mytho-poetic statements noted in his earlier article (1956a:9). "The main thesis is that the most significant Jewish and Christian texts are those in which the redemptive assurance and hope are brought to bear upon the totality of the human situation, including not only the individual soul but society, not only the party or sect or nation but all mankind, not only history but creation, and all focused upon the present *kairos* in its most circumstantial and somatic reality" (1958b:243). This criterion of significance presumes six "chief aspects of significant social symbol" (1958b:243). Such vital corporate symbols are group-binding, time-binding, immediately relevant, transcendentally open, explosively and cumulatively dramatic, and involving both emotion and cognition, both declaration and witness, both "wisdom and not merely excitement" (1958b:244).

The final article in this triad does indeed raise the wider or deeper question of language itself. "We must look to ultimate considerations about language itself and to the modes in which different apprehensions of reality come to speech" (1971a:439). But although this article avoids any appeal to mythic mentality, its major purpose is not fundamental grounding in linguistic philosophy. Its major concern is to continue exploring the *criterion of cosmic significance* as the discriminator not only within ancient eschatology (1958b) but especially between ancient and modern eschatology (1971a).

"Common to all true apocalyptic is a situation characterized by anomie, a loss of 'world,' or erosion of structures, psychic and cultural, with the consequent nakedness to Being or immediacy to the dynamics of existence. Hence the rhetorics of this 'panic' exposure in which all is at stake, involving antinomies of life and death, light and darkness, knowledge and nescience, order and chaos. And it can never be only a question of the individual. It is a juncture which renews the archaic crisis of existence: that of survival, the viability of life" (1971a:440–41). With that basic principle Wilder's next step is to discuss the rhetoric of ontological panic. "If we then identify the matrix of apocalyptic language with situations of anomie, what special kinds of rhetoric will we expect to find? What is the linguistic gesture of the zero-point, granting that such an expression is hyperbolic? I would like to press my point that in such occasions meaning can come through only in enigmatic ciphers drawn from outside the immediate cultural heritage" (1971a:444). Granting, of course, that the communal nature of language makes any absolute discontinuity unutterable and granting, equally, that radical discontinuity is disconcerting enough in any case, Wilder argues that "the hierophany in this situation calls forth, as it were, nonlanguage, or rhetorics featured by enormity and paradox. In this situation of disorientation, vertigo, and weightlessness there are not only no answers; there are no categories, no questions" (1971a:444). It is not clear how we should interpret Wilder's emphasis on "group hierophany": is it granted to an individual but for and in a group or directly to that group itself? Neither is it clear how far we should press ecstatic acclamation over against oral or even written art in this entire phenomenon. But he is surely correct to insist that it is this "situation of broken continuities" (1971a:447) where "*all* was forfeit to chaos" (1971a: 447–48) that best explains the "archaic and acultural character of the rhetorics" and that best explains "the large role played by the nonhuman world, the imagery drawn from the inanimate order: stone, mountain, tree, fire, celestial bodies, meteorology; as well as from mythical theriology: dragon, beasts, insects" (1971a: 448).

Wilder's judgment on modern apocalyptic writings (Nathaniel West's *The Day of the Locust,* John Barth's *The Sot-Weed Factor,* Thomas Pynchon's *V)* is that they "focus only on the negative or catastrophic aspect" (1971a:450). Their vision is not sufficiently "total, cosmic, and ultimate" and it lacks "the phase of miraculous renovation and that world affirmation which has gone through the experience of world negation. A hierophany properly means both Nay-saying and Yea-saying, and the catastrophic imagination alone is therefore not genuinely apocalyptic" (1971a:451). In a beautifully appropriate misprint the text twice speaks of cultural "inconoclasm" (1971a:441, 452), and Wilder underlines very well the modern lure of cheap eschatology and the contemporary call of apocalyptic chic. His warning is indeed both timely and timeless (1971a:440):

> One should be able to tell the difference between the tantrums of a romantic who cannot bring the world to heel and the impersonal voice which speaks out of the crucible where the world is made and unmade. In both ancient and modern apocalyptic we recognize bastard exemplars, not deeply rooted in man's ultimate *aporia* but animated by some partisan grievance, or lacking in vitality in keeping with a schizoid departure from reality. In such cases the rhetoric moves toward the monological and towards manic fantasy. Yet the recurrence of "ranters," alarmists, and purveyors of 'florid extremism' should not blind us to the healthy function of genuine transcendental apocalyptic.

But when all that is said, it is also possible that our twentieth-century world-loss is far more devastating than that of the first century and that we shall have to accept many partial and incomplete visions instead of one magnificently adequate one. It may even be that the plurality of their incompletions is our only possible totality, our only present wholeness.

CHAPTER 2
LITERATURE AND BIBLE

In a rural Sunday School class taught by a village housewife in ways surely contrary to all the precepts of the religious educator, the parable of the Sower was the theme, no doubt assigned in some long since repudiated graded lesson book. I was fourteen at the time, and my reaction my have been colored by the fact that I was working on a farm that summer. In any case I have always recalled with wonder the impact, the imaginative reverberations and the psychic dynamics of the six verses of the parable . . . This revelatory power of the parable was no doubt related to the fresh sensibility of childhood, but the experience has always remained with me as one of my earliest memories of the power of Scripture and of language generally.

(1974b:135–36)

I'm old-fashioned in the sense that my initial orienting vision of things came out of the Biblical shaping, the roots and personal experience, at that time in life, you know, when you're seventeen or eighteen or twenty-five when these things are pretty irreversible. They shape your outlook, your categories, your future experience. That was determinative for me in any case. But *always*, this anchorage in tradition was unhappy unless it could establish *humanist relationships* of all kinds: with the classics, with art and literature, with nature and the love of nature.

(1978b:17–18)

In over fifty years of publications Wilder both maintained that dialectic of biblical eschatology and social ethics and simultaneously broadened it to the wider polarities of literature and bible. And to this arena he brought certain gifts and advantages still unmatched in American experience.

There are several major scholars associated with the interdisciplinary area known as religion and literature in America. Most of these writers proceed from a background in which religious consciousness is disciplined primarily by philosophical theology. Wilder's first advantage is that religion for him is primarily mediated through biblical theology, that is, religion and literature start by being together and are united in the biblical tradition itself. He does not start from a bifurcated consciousness of philosophical theology and artistic literature and thereafter struggle to harmonize them. He starts from their interaction and confronts all other literary and religious works with his archetypal combination. A second major advantage is that most of the religion and literature scholars seem peculiarly frightened of the Bible. Instead of turning their interdisciplinary competence on the Bible as itself the combination of religion and literature, they prefer to stay away from it. But Wilder, clearly, has no such fear. Above all, of course, there is the third advantage that he had published two books of poetry (1923, 1928) before he ever finished his doctoral dissertation (1933). And in over fifty years of writing he has published about as many books of poems as of biblical commentary or of literary criticism. Thus the phrase *biblical literature,* ordinarily used with prejudicial emphasis on one term over the other, is perfectly appropriate to describe Wilder's major concern. Starting from the unity of *biblical literature* he has always been equally at home in the *biblical* and the *literary*. Indeed, he has said of his fourth book of poetry that "these poems may be seen as the pursuit in another genre of my work as a student of the New Testament" (1972a:xi), so that even his poetry and his exegesis are but two facets of the one phenomenon.

In the two decades when Wilder was teaching at Chicago (1943–1954) and at Harvard (1954–1963) he published three books of literary criticism and another three of biblical interpretation. The first two (1940a, 1952), on literature, were written mostly at the Wilder's summer home in Blue Hill, Maine. The next two (1954c, 1955), on the Bible, were derived primarily from guest lectures during the academic year. The last two, one on literature (1958c) and the other on the Bible (in 1964, but as 1971b), were both derived from guest lecture series. This process of intercalation between works on literature and works on the Bible graphically illustrates Wilder's dialectic of literary criticism and biblical commentary throughout this entire period. These six books will form the armature of the present chapter and shorter writings will be clustered around this sixfold interaction. My six section headings are taken from either the titles, subtitles, or prefaces of these six volumes and it is obvious that they are all variations on the single theme of the Bible and literature.

The first volume of literary criticism (1940a) was dedicated to his wife Catharine Kerlin, a 1929 Smith graduate whom he had met in 1929 and 1934 at Geneva. They were married in 1935 when she had returned from the International School there. The second book of biblical criticism (1955) was dedicated to their two children, Catharine Dix and Amos Tappan, who were born in 1937 and 1940.

2.1   Spirituality and Poetry

Although Wilder had published two books of poetry (1923, 1928) and his biblical dissertation (in 1939: see 1978a) by the thirties, he had published little on literary criticism before his volume *The Spiritual Aspects of the New Poetry* (1940a). But two book reviews published in the late thirties give indications of what would be important in that later volume.

In reviewing William L. Sperry's book *Wordsworth's Anti-Climax* (1935) Wilder suggested that it was necessary to "make a bolder evaluation of Wordsworth's religion" in explaining "'the most dismal anti-climax of which the history of literature holds record'" (1935:1146). And in suggesting what was lacking to Wordsworth's religion and to Sperry's analysis, Wilder offers that "smelting of the heart" and specifically mentions Dante as an example of it. Here, then, from the very beginning is Wilder's model for the ideal fusion of spirituality and poetry, of religious faith and artistic vision. A glance at the number of citations of Dante in the Index of his later book (1940a) reveals immediately that, as Virgil was for Dante, so Dante will always be for Wilder, *il miglior fabbro*.

A second review concerned a study by C. John McCole of, among others, Hemingway, Dos Passos, and Faulkner (1937b). The book's title is quite succinct: *Lucifer at Large*. Wilder's contention is that "it is possible, however, for one who pretends to judge this output from a Christian point of view both to applaud the critic in this case and to defend the writers." Noting that the author's models of literature are such works as *Gone with the Wind* or *Anthony Adverse*, and that his clear preference is for historical romance, Wilder says that, "thoughtful contemporary readers are often tired of reading stories, even good ones. They are tired of some types of brave souls that for all their courage have no curiosities, and they are tired of certain giants in the earth that have no subtlety, and in general of stories and story-writers that do not seem to know that the molds are broken today, not only the outer patterns but the deeper molds." Mercifully omitting McCole and his brutal title, Wilder took that review bodily into his first volume of literary criticism (1937b, 1940a:167–68).

Wilder proposes three major interests in this book (1940a:x–xi). The first purpose is "finding what light the new poetry throws upon the religious and ethical attitudes of men today, especially those not identified with the older traditions." The second objective is to understand, "given these attitudes, these features of the new poetry, what is their soil?" And the final focus is to access "the outlook of these poets and those among moderns for whom they speak." Wilder is concerned with poets such as "T.S. Eliot, Ezra Pound, Robinson Jeffers, Eugene O'Neill, A. MacLeish, Conrad Aiken, Hart Crane, E.E. Cummings, D.H. Lawrence, W.H. Auden, Kenneth Patchen" (1940a:4), critics like "Allen Tate, John Crowe Ransom, Yvor Winters, T.S. Eliot and others" (1940a:xvi), and his appended "Orientation and Reading Guide" (1940a:235–49) gives basic biographical and bibliographical data on the writers under discussion.

Although it does not appear in the book's terminal Index, the theme of "negation" runs almost like a refrain throughout this study. The word is used over thirty times, from as early as page xi to as late as page 228, and appears as often as three times on certain pages (1940a: 27, 58). It also appears in "Factors Making for Negation" as the title of one of the book's three sections (1940a:49–109). In noting the words Wilder most usually associates with "negation," it is rather clear that the term has extremely pejorative connotations. Examples are, "widespread negation not to say spiritual demoralization" (1940a:xi), "despair and negation" (1940a:64), "disillusion and negation" (1940a:73), "negation and decadence" (1940a:84), "negation or disarray" (1940a:161). The opposites of "negation" are also indicative of this pejorative understanding. Examples are "faith and negation" (1940a:xiii), and the comment that "we will have greater religious poetry when the devout and mystical poets among us enter as deeply into the experience of grace as our poets of negation enter into the experience of perdition" (1940a:44). There are also, however, a few places where "negation" points in a more positive direction. Wilder considers that the "sense of spiritual insecurity in modern poetry, while it prompts to negation, nevertheless has the merit of depth" (1940a:8); that it is "one of the merits of modern poetry that it at least bears witness to the dimensions of life, if only in negative terms" (1940a:54); and that "negation in the form of pessimism or bitterness is far from fulfilling the condition of religious insight. Negation in the form of the tragic view is not far from the kingdom of Heaven" (1940a:58). But it is clear above all that, for Wilder, one must pass beyond or through negation to affirmation. Thus he speaks "of those truly modernist poets who have come through a modernist negation and emerged with a positive outlook, still in the modernist temper" (1940a:27), and he judges that T.S. Eliot "reached beyond his contemporary dilemmas to triumphant affirmation" (1940a: 41). Here already areas which will demand future development and specification are becoming obvious. Even, or especially, if a poet's work is pessimistic or nihilistic when taken as didactic content, does not the very act of publishing composed and written poetry, be it flawed or flaming, represent itself an act of affirmation, contradicting by the challenge of the form the very substance of the content? Is not, in other words, the problem of negation and affirmation more subtle than it might at first appear and might it not apply as much to form as to content, to style as to substance? Twenty years later Wilder wrote an article on St.-John Perse entitled "The Modern Wrestle with the Negation" (1962d); but the term, while still rather pejorative (246: "unjustified negation"), is not probed any more deeply than in 1940.

Wilder wishes "to engage a certain conversation with the new schools of both poets and critics over issues of ethics and world view that appear in their work" (1940a:xv), but in this conversation Wilder does not speak as himself a poet but rather "in terms of what has been called classical Christianity" (1940a:xi). There is nothing wrong with this, of course, but since Wilder is both poet and theologian, it is fascinating to wonder what would have happened if he had spoken as a poet to poets, even as a poet of affirmation to poets of negation, rather than as a theologian. One would never know from this book that Wilder had already published two books of poetry. He cites himself only once, without naming the poem and almost in passing (1940a:66), and only the presence of his *Arachne* (1928) among the "Poets" in the terminal Bibliography (1940a:256) lets one discover the cited poem as "Annals of Circumstances and Beauty: Sonnets" (1928:27, see also 1943a:50). No doubt there are certain protocols involved in being poet and critic, and in citing one's own poetry when criticizing other poets. Still, the silent existence of Wilder's two books raises interesting questions, one on form and one on content. He admits "I was one of those who had little acquaintance with the many forms of 'modern' poetry until a dozen years ago" (1940a:x), that is, presumably, until after his two books of poetry had already appeared (1923, 1928). This would mean that Wilder's earlier poetry was written without knowing, in the words of Peter Munro Jack reviewing this 1940a volume in *The New York Times Book Review* for July 7, 1940, "the new, vital and really contemporary poetry, though Ezra Pound had been writing since 1909 ('Personae') and Eliot's 'Prufrock' was being read in 1917."

But, turning to content, an even more interesting question arises. Early and late in this book Wilder notes that "what distinguishes them all as moderns is that they write as those who have lived since the flood — that is, since the World War and in general man's latter dis-illusioning discoveries of himself" (1940a:18–19), and again, "the con-sequent strifes, especially the World War and its aftermath, have disabused many men of their older patriotic and religious loyalties" (1940a:218). And as an example of "the somberness of mind of those who have met the war conditions of our epoch at first hand" (1940a: 74), Wilder cites explicitly the "experience of MacLeish the ex-soldier" (1940a:76). Wilder, too, is both poet and ex-soldier. But again there is only a hint of this. "For our part, it seems to us that we met with Leviathan in the thickets of Villers-Cotterets in 1918" (1940a:28). The hint, however, leads directly to Wilder's own poem, "Armageddon. *Forêt de Villers-Cotterets, July 18, 1918*," (1928:45–49). Here, however, the experience of World War I is exhilarating, and the aftermath of war is martial rather than moral anti-climax (1928:49):

> To die was naught: we companied with the dead
> They died who came back to this blinder life.
> ....
> They died who came back to this blinder scene
> And woke to know the solar year again.

This is no passing isolated moment of inadvertant romanticism. The same thought in similar duplex format concluded "Battle-Retrospect," the poem which opened Wilder's first book of poetry (1923:7–10):

How are we fallen from our high estate
Who saw the dawn at Soissons that July
....
How are we fallen on another day
Whose life was a perpetual sacrament.

Wilder has acknowledged "that readers today may be puzzled, if not scandalized, by this theme of the prestige of the war experience and its imaginative overtones" (1968a:352), and again, that those who read his 1923 volume of war poems "may well be scandalized by the nostalgia there expressed" (1978b:34). Be that as it may, what might have happened in 1940 if Wilder as poet-veteran of World War I, having seen both ends of the shell—first as ambulance driver and then as artillery corporal, had confronted his own war poetry of affirmation with those others whose war poetry was of negation? Are there even affirmations requiring far severer ethical judgments than any negations? And what has Soissons to do with Patmos?

These questions recur in reading Wilder's comments on Yeats in this book and in two other writings from that same year which consider Yeats' later and final work (1940c, 1940d). One might wonder if there is a mixture of the pagan and the Christian in Wilder's war poetry, a mixture of "Aeschylean shade" (1923:8) and "Aeschylean mood" (1923:41) with "the frontier of God" (1928:42) and "the lists of God" (1928:48). Wilder passes a similar judgment on Yeats. He judges him "of that perennial race of the pagans who look to nature and the imagination for their faith" (1940a:203) and yet finds "beneath a formal rejection of it is a tacit appropriation of much" of Christianity (1940a: 533). Again, after insisting that "Yeats was first of all a religious poet, and he went all lengths to defend the rights of the spirit in a scientific and secularist age," he concludes that, "while Yeats was not a Christian, he can remind us of attitudes, liberties and mysteries of the spirit that our prevailingly unimaginative Christianity has lost sight of, and whose disciplines we refuse. Though some of the insensibilities of his paganism appear . . . he yet demonstrates, like Dante in one respect, how great an impulse even scorn can be to lift men into exceptional stature" (1940d).

Wilder maintains that "one school of the new writers should not be included in the cult of negation. This is the group whose concern is with social revolution" (1940a:178). His chapter on revolutionary poetry focuses especially on Kenneth Patchen and this entire section was reprinted much later in a volume dedicated to that poet (1977:123–35). The pages on Patchen himself also appeared in *Poetry* magazine (1940b). Wilder was criticized by Dudley Fitts, discussing his book for *Saturday Review of Literature* 22/16 (August 10, 1940), because the reviewer thought "he exaggerates the importance of a writer like

Patchen . . . who is treated with as much deference as Auden or Crane" (pp. 22–23). Nevertheless, and comparisons aside, Patchen's poetry and Patchen's life, including a quarter century of crippling spinal pain, best corroborates Wilder's statement that "if a critic loves and understands men he will not confuse the abiding ills of life nor his personal griev- ances with the ills of a particular social order. He will then be able to pass an illuminating judgment on his day" (1940a:195).

2.2   Christianity and Culture

In the period between his first (1940a) and second book (1952) of literary criticism, and against the background situation of war and immediate post-war restoration, Wilder participated in the annual meet- ings of the Conference on Science, Philosophy, and Religion in their Relation to the Democratic Way of Life, at Columbia University and the Jewish Theological Seminary in New York. He also contributed papers to their Second (1942b), Fifth (1945), Tenth (1950a), and Thirteenth Symposia (1954b). These same interests led also to the Institute for Religious and Social Studies and the publication of his article on "Literary Sources" in its volume *Foundations of Democracy* (1947a). It is significant that he himself cited this study as "Literary Sources of Freedom" and the book as *Foundations of Freedom* in a later article (1948b:25, note 7). Whether change of title or lapse of memory is involved in this difference, it was freedom that was always the focus of Wilder's interest.

Before America entered the war, Wilder, discussing "Social issues in contemporary poetry," asked, "Are the events taking place in Europe due to particular conditions over there? Are we perhaps only confront- ing a passing thunder storm in our western world, and may we expect to see the skies brighten suddenly after a short time, and our customary world-outline reappear? How tenacious are our best traditions of faith, character and sacrifice? In other words, what elements of soundness and social health may we bank on when danger threatens?" (1941b:3). Later, after America was at war, he denied any Christian imperative of pacifism (1943b) and, reviewing a book by George Bernanos, he claimed that "parts of the book represent prophetic political writing of the first order. It is strange that there has been so little adequate analysis of the events of our times. An American must feel a certain bitterness that no similar truth has been written about our case in these recent years, with a comparable force" (1944a:530).

At the end of the war Wilder himself asked "Is it possible from a Christian point of view, to interpret the war, not only negatively—i.e., as a judgment—but positively? Without seeing it as a crusade can we read a positive meaning into it that can in some measure minister to the bewilderment of many and satisfy their hunger for a deeper understanding of the costs involved?" (1945–46:76). He begins his answer on World War II from World War I. He notes that "the general consensus is that our men saw the war mainly or only as an ugly job that had to be cleared up as fast as possible so that they could get home" (1945–46:80). In contrast to that situation, "it is my testimony that in his heart of hearts the doughboy of that war, 'the unknown soldier'—though inarticulate about such matters—had his own tacit idealism and his own confused commitment, and it was this that had everything to do with the whole spirit of our American action and participation" (1945–46:81). This statement was important enough for Wilder to repeat it about twenty years later: "I take this occasion to testify that our indeed inarticulate common soldiers so far from their native ground had, nevertheless, a sense of being willing actors in a necessary drama and one inseparably linked with the meaning of the American story" (1968a:355). Although he is usually diffident about citing his own poetry in his critical writings, Wilder here quotes three of them (1945–46:81, 82, 85): first, to recall how the 1920 repudiation of Wilson ignored "the suffrage of the dead and the unborn" (1923:46); second, to honor those who "descend where the nethermost piers of history are building" (1943a:19); and, third, to suggest that "these infinite tasks are portents of a Work" (1943a:17). It is this "Work" from World War I experience that Wilder now offers as his own positive interpretation of World War II. "We begin to see that the great struggle of our age was not that between the Axis powers and the United Nations. No, the deeper struggle is that between an old world that is dying, and a new world that is coming to birth by the power of God" (1945–46:86–87). There is thus "a common impulse among the peoples of the world, a reaching out toward more liberty and a more abundant life." His understanding of the situation is that "we are the witnesses in our days of the birth pangs of a new order, indeed. It needs to come in the totalitarian states. And our overthrow of their present masters hastens it. And it needs to come in the Allied Nations and in the democracies. It needs to come here in our midst. And the tragedies of this apocalyptic hour—the costs at the front and the cost in the homes of our towns and cities—the public disasters and the private anguish—the convulsions of peoples and the endurances of individuals—all this *can* be the birth pangs of the Peoples' Peace" (1945–46:87–88).

In the early fifties Wilder recalled how, "soon after the recent war Robert Hutchins, then chancellor of the University of Chicago, initiated an exchange of professors between this institution and the University of Frankfurt. It was important at that time to draw the German universities out of their isolation, and there were those who felt that the first official approaches of our military government to German 're-education' were not altogether felicitous" (1953a:738). Wilder himself was an exchange professor for modern English-language poetry there in the spring term of 1950–1951 and the winter term of 1951–1952. He discussed his own experiences in the article just cited and went on to consider the "Moral Aspects of German Recovery" in an article for *Religion and Life* (1953b). He was in Germany when he learned that the manuscript of his book *Modern Poetry and the Christian Tradition* (1952) had been awarded the Bross Decennial Award administered by the Trustees of Lake Forest College in Illinois.

The purpose of that book is summed up in its epigraph, which is also one of Wilder's favorite aphorisms: "Test the spirits whether they are of God" (1 John 4:1). His thesis "is that the custody and future of the Christian tradition has to a considerable degree passed over into the keeping of non-ecclesiastical and even secular groups" (1952:xii). Because of this rather surprising situation, he intends to study "the vitality and operation of the Christian tradition, the work of the Holy Spirit, in our contemporary world, especially in its secularized aspects. Thus our particular topic is set in the larger frame of the relation of the church to contemporary culture. The field of observation we choose is that of modern poetry, the poetry, that is, which reflects our modern crisis" (1952:xv).

The book has three sections. The first three chapters present the historical and cultural background necessary to understand what is to follow. The next three chapters discuss the relationship between traditional and modern poetry. The last five chapters focus directly on contemporary poetry, and Wilder is here "concerned to distinguish the poetry of Catholic, Anglican and Protestant background and inspiration in assessing the artistic fertility of the Christian tradition today" (1952:xv–xvi).

In giving historical background Wilder admits that "there is much truth in the view that the story of the modern world is that of a great adventure in self-sufficiency which has brought it nemesis, meanwhile offering us a varied display of heretical and watered-down Christianity along the way" (1952:40). But this negative analysis is not completely adequate to the situation. Instead, "our positive appreciation of many of the modern poets and the modern movement in literature and the arts, beginning with certain of the romantic school, rests on the view that they represent pioneering impulses occasioned by the limitations of 'orthodoxy,' so contributing to a new Christian formulation and pattern" (1952:42). And one of the major limitations of orthodoxy is a misunderstanding of its own language. "The Christian faith must not, indeed, be dissolved into 'myth' or into 'poetry.' It rests on unrepeatable and decisive historical events and its formulations include an essential intellectual content. But dogma is always mythopoetic and not discursive." Thus he concludes that "we may go on to say, by way of parable, that the Deity is a poet rather than a mathematician. His dealing with the world is an epic poem as his redemption action is a drama. And man's primary response is a psalm, a lyric, a doxology" (1952:20).

In relating traditional and modern poetry Wilder speaks of "the sea of new forces and the islands of surviving order," and he argues that "these islands of security are rapidly shrinking and that a general transformation is rapidly taking place in our whole culture and way of life" (1952:75–76). This is why Wilder places himself, although with a certain nostalgia, on the side of the moderns. "When the bonds of an old culture are dissolved the insecurities and anguish of rootlessness and estrangement, as we have seen, lead men to various forms of new order and new faith. In such a moment the most significant poetry will arise out of the depths of the disarray rather than out of the compromised citadels of tradition or out of the tentative new homes of the spirit" (1951:75). Wilder then proceeds to test all this and by "adducing these examples of the work of Norman Nicholson, Dylan Thomas and St.-John Perse, we have sought to suggest in this one area, the treatment of nature, that the method and scope of the traditional poet is subject to special limitations. The modern crisis when felt in its depth transforms the vision of nature as well as man and the modern resources of prosody lend themselves to this new vision to make possible new ranges of utterance" (1951:11).

The section on modern poetry takes up the second half of the volume, and Wilder structures his analysis on a first century parallel. In the relationship between primitive Christianity and its surrounding world "there were three possible solutions. One group of the early Christians wished to Judaize, to retain the existing Jewish-Christian patterns of belief and cult. Another group took the course of 'acute Hellenization,' that is, of taking over the forms of paganism to such a point that it surrendered the substance of the faith. Out from between these two extremes finally emerged the early Catholic church" (1951: 178). This threefold typology guides Wilder's judgment on the responses of Christianity to modernity. "The Roman church we may say 'Judaizes' in the sense that it withholds itself from full involvement in the forces that have made the modern situation. On the other wing, we have 'acute Hellenization' in the sense today of 'acute secularization.' This includes all those especially Protestant elements which have allowed themselves to be taken over by modern movements and ideologies, rationalistic, romantic, neo-pagan, Marxist, or a combination of these. In between we have the central stream of Protestantism and Anglo-Catholicism" (1952:179).

But whatever value these generalities may have on official and ecclesiastical levels, it is not clear that they assist one's reading of the individual poets concerned. Gerard Manley Hopkins, for example, rightly judged a "superb poet" (1952:12), is the only figure given a whole chapter to himself (1952:148–75) and is thus of special interest to Wilder. One might easily question certain disciplines imposed by his religious vocation and might even question more forcibly his own interpretation of those disciplines' application: compare, for instance, Ignatius of Loyola's saying on page 171 that "we do not for our own part wish . . . for honor rather than dishonor" with Hopkin's comment on page 172 that "it is holier to be unknown than to be known." But Wilder concludes that "his vocation made the struggle more acute and imposed highly restrictive barriers upon the artistic activity ensuing, but at the same time thereby intensified it" (1952:167). Thus, later, when Wilder maintains, for both Hopkins and Eliot, that "the Christian heritage in its Catholic frame has too formal a character to enter into full encounter with modern experience" (1952:279), one must still wonder whether the Catholic poet's struggle is as much empowered as impoverished by that against which he must struggle even within his own tradition and discipline. What Jacob needs a crippled angel?

But, in any case, Wilder's analysis maintains that "W.H. Auden, who is a very Protestant kind of Anglo-Catholic, takes on a representative significance" (1952:196) in the contemporary situation. Twenty-five years later it was precisely this section on Auden (1952:196–204) which was chosen for inclusion in a book of essays on *Religion and Modern Literature* (1975b). This representative function of Auden consists in the fact that there "are children of the church who have been caught up in the dilemma of the age, who are struggling at first hand with its major heresies, and whose faith is 'for the time being' uncrystallized . . . A relevant and powerful version of Christianity for the time to come will emerge as much from the explorations of such prodigals as from the stay-at-homes of the tradition, as the case of Auden himself shows" (1952:204).

2.3   Transcendence and Escapism

If Wilder had been willing to criticize modern poetry for refusing the assistance of available Christian resources (1940a, 1952), he was equally willing to turn around and criticize contemporary Christianity for rendering unintelligible or irrelevant the profoundest depths of those very same resources. His next two books, therefore, moved to the biblical rather than the literary pole of the dialectic considered throughout this present chapter.

Between these next two books (1954c, 1955), Wilder joined the faculty of the Harvard Divinity School so that that former work took "occasion to acknowledge my gratitude to my colleagues during these past years in the Chicago Theological Seminary and in the Federated Theological Faculty of the University" (1954c:10). One of the last articles produced from Chicago derived from Wilder's participation with

"The Chicago Committee" in preparing "Ecumenical Biblical Studies."
His own subject was "The New Society in the New Age" (1954e).

The next book *Otherworldliness and the New Testament* (1954c) arose
from Wilder's Jackson Lectures at the Perkins School of Theology in
Dallas during February, 1954, and his Schaffer Lectures at Yale Divinity
School in April, 1954. His thesis is that "the one great and telling
accusation made against the Christian religion in our modern period is
that it is 'escapist,' that it evades responsibility for the problems of our
life in this world . . . that the Christian conviction of things not seen
and the Resurrection hope mean escapism, pie-in-the-sky, the opium of
the people, what they call 'compensatory fictions'" (1954c:18–19). This
problem is a familiar starting point for Wilder. When he had been
invited, for example, along with Arnold Toynbee and C.S. Lewis to
comment on "The Christian Hope: Its Meaning for Today" by *Religion
in Life*, he started by noting that "it is supposed that the future state as
anticipated by Christians represents merely a kind of adventitious re-
ward, a consolation prize for ills of this life" (1951b:11).

The book confronts this accusation of irrelevant otherworldliness in
three specific areas, that of New Testament theology, of the historical
Jesus, and of the resurrectional hope. But before focusing on these individual areas, Wilder insists that "religion in the Bible roots in man's
primordial impulses and social bonds" (1954c:31), so that its "stories lay
bare the roots of human vitality, the cables which carry the powerful
voltage of human impulse and action, whether creative or destructive"
(1954c:36).

In arguing that contemporary New Testament theology carefully
avoids escapism, Wilder places most emphasis on *kerygma* and on
Heilsgeschichte. In an earlier discussion of *Heilsgeschichte* he had been
willing to term it "the most promising contemporary approach to the
task" of rendering New Testament theology understandable today
(1947b:435). He was also quite willing to suggest ways in which it
needed further development: "That story is a true story but like all true
stories it can be falsified by insensitive repetition or by incurious
acquiescence" (1948c:17). Here he is again cautious about it, and his
primary concern is that "too exclusive an emphasis on the *kerygma* . . .
tends to narrow the meaning of what it is to be a Christian," that is,
"what God did in Christ was more than announce a message; it was to
bring a new kind of community to birth, to effect a new social creation"
(1954c:55). This means that even *kerygma* or *Heilsgeschichte* can only
work today when they touch a person "at the level where he has been
seared or terrified or haunted" (1954c:59).

In the chapter on the historical Jesus, Wilder's "main concern is to
recognize a measure of human reality, indeed of sociological reality, in
the figure of the Nazarene; to identify a real protagonist in a real this-
worldly drama; to invite attention to a realm of second-causes in the

working of God; and so to arrest the impulse to docetism which otherwise has a free field for itself" (1954c:82).

A digression. In 1943 the periodical *Motive* had asked various writers, including William Faulkner, to discuss Jesus as "The Man Who Looked like God." Wilder chose to "offer as a clue to the picture of Jesus as he might appear today the following story, retold from the French of Georges Duhamel, one of the great writers of our time. I insist that it is only a clue, only a parable, but I think one may learn more from it than from many direct attempts to delineate the features of the Man of Nazareth" (1943c:13). In the midst of the Second World War Wilder retells the *Elevation et Mort d'Armand Branche* published by Duhamel right after the First World War (Paris: Grasset, 1919). Armand Branche arrived as a replacement on the French front at Roye and Lassigny in the late winter of 1916–1917. "As they worked with him, the other men of the squad noted that he had fits of abstraction and a kind of simple-mindedness that made them tap their heads sometimes and wink at one another. But they couldn't help liking him. There was something tender and humble in the corner of his mouth. Besides he would talk to the *poilus* about their homes, their wives, their children" (1943c:14). Then, "one bright morning as the sun was rising," and as signs of the coming French counter-attack multiplied to his rear, Armand Branche climbed out of his trench, advanced towards the barbed wire, and, clearly visible to both sides, shouted out his message: "You go home, and we'll go home, and it will all be over. Go on back and we'll have peace!" (1943c:14). Badly wounded by an immediate machine-gun response, Branche lingered for days in a field hospital barely this side of death. Then came news from the front. The Germans were gone. Gone from the front-line, the second-line, and even the third-line trenches. The event, known to history as "the famous German withdrawal of March, 1917," vacated a fifty-mile stretch of front north of Lassigny. And north of Armand Branche who, on hearing of it, died with "a look on his face so poignant and tender that the orderly thought that if there is a God he must have a look like that" (1943c:15). End of a digression.

So also, in this chapter on the historical Jesus, Wilder insists that Jesus is "a stranger and an alien to our day; that his thinking was not as our thinking, and his language not as our language" (1954c:73). But although Wilder maintains that Jesus' "summons represented a real alternative to Jews a generation before the catastrophe that fell upon the nation and which cast its shadow before" (1954c:90), the problems of criteria and corpus seen earlier in considering eschatology and ethics reappear here. What are the *criteria* whereby "we can penetrate back behind Matthew's discourse" (1954c:87, note 15) or that of the other evangelists? And what precisely is the *corpus* of words and deeds, aphorisms and narratives, actions and conflicts obtained by such criteria and on which alone a total picture of the historical Jesus might be established?

The book's final chapter concerns that contemporary relevance of resurrectional faith. He notes how "Rudolf Bultmann has sought to give meaning to the Resurrection of Christ for modern man in a much discussed proposal . . . Those, he says, who consent to be crucified with Christ awaken with him to God's new creation. They recognize his Resurrection *at one and the same time* that they themselves rise to newness of life. That Christ rose from the dead was and is revealed to faith alone, not to the unbelieving. Thus, on this view, *the Resurrection is the other side of the Cross when the Cross is looked on in faith*" (1954c:98–99). Although Wilder is somewhat hesitant about the proposal's "existential and otherworldly formulation" (1954c:100), he is quite sympathetic to it and offers no alternative to its substance. Besides the argument that the crucified Jesus was visible to belief and disbelief while the risen Lord was visible only to faith, there is also the argument from the univalence of crucifixion narrative as compared with the polyvalence of resurrectional apparition with regard to time and place, receiver and reception, mandate and mission. Wilder does not use this second argument although he had laid the groundwork for it by his earlier article on "Variant Traditions of the Resurrection in Acts" (1943d).

The book's overall conclusion recalls what Wilder said about the Revised Standard Version of the New Testament in *The Atlantic Monthly* for December, 1946. There he had noted that we "may well be warned by the great principle of Tertullian, 'Christ our Master called himself truth not custom'" (1946b:142). He concludes the present volume with the hope "that the talent entrusted to us is not diverted from its proper circulation and productivity by being wrapped safely in a napkin, even in a napkin of the most hallowed and cherished uses and associations" (1954c:122).

2.4   Faith and Modernity

The next volume to be considered among the six which structure the present chapter is *New Testament Faith Today*. Four of its six chapters (I, III, IV, V) are a "much expanded and rewritten" (1955:9) version of lectures for the School of Religion at Butler University in 1948 which had originally appeared in *The Shane Quarterly* (1948d). Another chapter (II) had also been published before but elsewhere (1954b), and a final chapter (VI) was added when all of this was published as a book (1955).

The problem posed for the book is the same as that confronted in the preceding volume (1954c). "The interpreter of the Bible today must reconcile two somewhat different tasks. He must make clear how alien its assumptions and conceptions are from those of today, thus safeguarding major insights, however much of scandal they may involve for modern thinking. Next, from this point of vantage or disadvantage he must seek to convey this body of thought and faith in the most persuasive way possible to a different age" (1955:9). This problem (I) and its solution (II) are then tested in interpretation of Jesus (III), Paul (IV), and John (V).

As he formulates his problem, what we would today term the hermeneutical question, Wilder reverts again to *Heilsgeschichte,* but now it seems clear that "salvation-history" is less a contemporary reinterpretation than a contemporary reiteration of the Bible's own mythical language. "The whole world story could not be charted then as a circle, a cycle or a spiral, nor, indeed, as an ascending line. Neither, indeed, could it be represented by a jagged line of crests and troughs, but rather as a letter U. Descent and ascent. A fall and a restoration. Lost and found. Paradise Lost and Paradise Regained. The whole history of the world was like the story of the prodigal son or like the story of Joseph" (1955:28). *Heilsgeschichte* is not only *like a story,* it is like one very special type of story, it is like a fable, fairy story, or children's tale. "This theology of history, in terms of lost and found, has all the simplicity of a children's tale. We are reminded of a recurrent pattern or plot in old folktales: ordeal and triumph, banishment and restoration, humiliation and glory, feud and reconciliation. The universal appeal in such fables lies in the fact that we think we recognize our own story in them" (1955:29). These analogies are very significant for they entail the extension of mythology not merely to thematic part but to structural whole in such a *Heilsgeschichte.* Thus Wilder acknowledges that it is precisely in this "mythopoetic world story" that "the modern interpreter meets here his greatest difficulty, since the truth value of the symbols used is so deeply compromised for us" (1955:30). That is, not only the parts but the whole, not only the elements but the structure, not only the units but the unity is mythopoetic and thus demands constant reinterpretation for new situations.

When the problem is stated as clearly as that, one is not surprised to find the name of Rudolf Bultmann invoked quite early in the second chapter. "Professor Rudolf Bultmann of Marburg has raised these questions in a thoroughgoing way in the course of his work on the New Testament during the last quarter century" (1955:41). But although Wilder is profoundly appreciative of Bultmann's "honesty in facing the problem" (1955:43), he is just as profoundly doubtful that his understanding of mythopoetic language is adequate for a solution. He had said this even earlier in a review: "Bultmann sees the myth as obsolete prescientific fiction . . . It is our view that mythopoetic language is an indispensable vehicle of the biblical truth and message. It does not grow obsolete though it is in need of constant interpretation and re-interpretation" (1950b:122). The same objection is raised here. "But the fundamental point is that mythology in the sense of imaginative presentation is essential in religion. The language of faith requires it and glories in it. The more vital the faith is the more inevitably its world vision projects itself in dramatic ritual" (1955:45). The core problem is that rationalism, positivism, and scientism are also mythical, the myth of the dispensability of myth, the myth of the denial of myth, and the myth of the obsolescence of myth. Wilder argues that "the chief obstacle to the proper validation of religious myth and all cognate mythopoetic portrayals of life and history is the stultifying axiom that genuine truth or insight or wisdom must be limited to that which can be stated in discursive prose, in denotative language stripped as far as possible of all connotative suggestions, in 'clear ideas,' in short, in statement or description of a scientific character" (1955:60). The polyvalence of mythopoetic language is its abiding power and as such it demands not demythologizing but interpretation, and this hermeneutic will have to apply to every part and to every level since "the New Testament is, of course, full of such symbol and mythopoetical language from beginning to end, from the single detail or metaphor through the parable, allegory, extended trope, legend (in the sense of hagiographic account), to mythical narrative (theophany, etc.), to all-encompassing world myth" (1955:64). With this understanding of mythopoetic language as his basis Wilder next considers the proclamation of Jesus, the message of Paul, and the witness of John.

He begins with Jesus "as the initial expression of that wave of faith which manifests itself in the entire New Testament and in Christianity down to our day" (1955:72). There is again no discussion of criteria or corpus for Jesus' proclamation, but Mark 1:15 is the chapter's epigraph and this summarizes the message of the historical Jesus (not the redactional Mark) for Wilder. "Jesus testifies that in his generation God is bringing in the new age, and this is a matter of good news and warning . . . And this was 'at hand.' It was coming soon and once-and-for-all. Indeed it was already making its power felt. It was already present in this sense" (1955:74, 75–76). The core problem is immediately and very accurately stated: "What concerns . . . in the case of Jesus' language about the kingdom is how far he spoke, as we say, 'literally,' and how far 'symbolically'" (1955:82). Wilder begins his answer with a distinction we have seen before (#1.4). "In this area the Jewish and early Christian language of faith and expectancy was neither literal nor consciously symbolic but, in its proper sense, naive" (1955:83, see 1956a:11). Once again, however, this key distinction is neither explained, exemplified, nor grounded in any theory of language or of literature. "Naive," one presumes, would be the state prior to the conscious distinction of "literal" and "symbolic," the state, for example, of the playing child? And one wonders immediately if that is a good description of the mind that created the parables, for example. In applying these distinctions to Jesus' language Wilder's first comments are quite radical. "We can learn something from the suggestion that Jesus 'saw eternity in an hour,' that he 'foreshortened history,' that *he transferred his sense of the nearness of God from the spiritual to the temporal order*, that a new creation did in a sense begin with his work, and that he used the parables of faith to convey the destiny of the world and of man" (1955:83, my italics). At this point it seems clear that symbolicity may apply not only to the *clouds* but the *coming*, not only to the *trumpet* but the *time*, not only to the *scenario* but even to the *Son of Man* himself. But then, as if somewhat frightened by the implications of this proposal, Wilder backs off from it. He cites Paul Minear's warning "in connection with such details of the judgment as the clouds of heaven, the earthquake motif, the last trumpet, how wrong it is to take these in a crassly literal fashion" (1955:86). But such treating of a myth as a menu is no longer tolerable once Wilder himself has made us aware that the problem is not the symbolicity of the *details* but of the general *judgment* itself. And he cites Oscar Cullmann's warning that realized eschatology in which "the kingdom . . . does not really refer to a future reality but to a present one" is "untrue . . . to the real time sense and hope of early Christianity" (1955:84). Wilder himself, however, has just proposed that this *time sense* itself may be symbolical or even prior to the distinction of literal and symbolical, that is, naive. One may note, in passing, the double use of "real" in discussing Cullmann above. We now have: literal, symbolic, naive, and real. Once again, the question must be pressed: does real mean literal or symbolic or naive, and how are these terms to be theoretically grounded? Still, Wilder's basic intuition is far too powerful for any such withdrawals. At the end of the chapter he repeats his basic contention "that the New Testament doctrine of the return of Christ (or Jesus' announcement of the coming of the Son of Man) belongs to the order of symbolic and mythopoetic statement and was not understood literally in the late Jewish and early Christian religion" (1955:104). Thus, even more forcibly than earlier, he maintains that the language was, and was understood to be, symbolic. And such symbolism refers not only to details of scenario but to the very phenomenon itself. The very *coming* is symbolic: "We must frankly concede that no such dramatic return of Christ with the clouds is to be expected in the course of history. He has his own way of coming but not this way" (1955:103). And so also is the *time* symbolic: "The kingdom of God is at hand — ever at hand, and in a degree ever within reach" (1955:106).

Turning to Paul, Wilder finds his epigraph and "key text of Paul in Romans 1:16, 17" (1955a:107). He considers Paul in strict continuity with Jesus so that "there is no gulf" between them. "They declare the same sublime fact — an unimaginable world transformation in course" (1955:108). Nevertheless, Paul does "stand on this side of the resurrection" (1955:111) and, thus, "lays great stress on Christ himself and especially on his cross and resurrection" (1955:117). But Paul also requires a "sharpened sense of moral inadequacy over against the august holiness of the Deity" (1955:112), and this explains his "strong emphasis on the negative aspects of the Gospel" (1955:117). In an earlier article on Paul, Wilder had claimed "that the Gospel prevailed because the Word of the Cross, a scandal to the Jew and foolishness to the Greek, *reached down to a new level in the human conscience and crystallized a new order of human relationships*" (1944b:186). So also here he claims that Paul "made appeal to their sleeping hungers and faiths, and cast a torch into the explosive damps of the soul, of the Jew first and then of the Greek" (1955:121). In so doing Paul was but continuing and widening the process whereby, "from the time of John the Baptist on, a crater had opened in the deeper life of mankind evidencing prodigious creative impulses, and the whole New Testament is the record of how the nature of men and their cultural forms, Jew and Greek, were baptized, smelted and transformed by the visitation" (1955:125). Against this general understanding as background Wilder admits, however, that "many features of Paul's message of salvation and judgment, if taken at face value, are no longer meaningful or available to us today: the imminent world end; the cosmology with its heavenly powers, the origin of sin and death in Adam" (1955:122). He singles out two features of this problem of reinterpretation for attention. There is, first, "the theme of substitutionary atonement" and he suggests that "in the absence of ample faith, the great images and concepts of Paul become shrunken and literal" (1955:109). Unfortunately, this subject is not developed any further so that the possibilities of "substitutionary atonement" as *symbolic* language are not explored. Wilder is primarily interested in how "redemption as Paul understood it had what we would call a political and cultural meaning" (1955:138). He develops this through a reinterpretation of those sayings in which Paul talks of God having dethroned the powers and principalities through the cross (Gal 4:3-4, 8-9, Col 2:15). We are aware today, terribly aware today, that "personal freedom is inexorably limited by massive impersonal legacies, social forms and dogmas which constitute fate for men and have as it were an existence of their own. This is what Paul was talking about in his own way in referring to the powers, principalities, and world rulers, although his thinking about them pursued them right down into their metaphysical roots" (1955:128). This is an extremely powerful interpretation of Paul's symbolic language and it opens up a huge area of his message which has no precise equivalent in Jesus' own symbolic message. Thus, Wilder concludes, "redemption involves the tyrants of the forum, the market place and the hearth; the false dogmas of the state and the economy; the idolatries and spells of social traditions as they appear in inflexible conventions and complacencies; and the insidious authorities of unreason and passion that speak through propaganda and the mass media. Here operate the principalities and powers that are potentially dethroned by Christ" (1955:140).

In turning to the Johannine witness, with John 12:31 and 1 John 5:4 as epigraph, Wilder acknowledges that the fourth gospel "makes an especial appeal to many modern men outside the churches and to many Christians who find Paul a stumbling block" (1955:142). Although Wilder does not suggest it, part of John's appeal may rest on the fact that his is a different interpretation of crucifixion-resurrection from that of Paul and that once there are two interpretations there can be others as well. Thus John's reinterpretation of the faith is itself a vindication of Wilder's claim that such is always needed, not only now but even then. There are two special facets of John's own restatement requiring special emphasis. "The conception of eternal life *here and now* largely supersedes the conception of the new age to come in the future. The conception of a present automatic judgment largely supersedes that of a future forensic last judgment. The conception of Christ's return after his death in the form of the Spirit largely supersedes that of his parousia on the clouds" (1955:148). It is not, of course, that John's language is itself to be taken literally and unsymbolically. But it is a different symbolism and seems indeed to be a quite deliberate rephrasing of one set of symbols into another. But besides this realized or mystical eschatology there is a second facet whereby John appeals to many moderns. "This Gospel, together with the First Epistle of John, moreover, sanctions a Christian freedom in all that concerns church, office and sacrament which is needed today. These writings were not only antignostic but they were also anti-ecclesiastical. The authority of the apostles is meaningfully subordinated to that of the 'beloved disciple' who is a symbol of the true witness of faith in any generation, whether an eye-witness of Christ or not" (1955:162–63). The scandal of universality in particularity, of a revelation located in history and claiming validity for all peoples and all languages, all times and all places, is still very much present in John, if anything even more so than in Paul. Yet even as our modernity reaches for scorn, it acknowledges that to dismiss such claims requires universally valid statements whose very possibility we are seeking to deny. Thus Wilder's summary statement that "the concentration of John's message is upon the love and glory of God as they come to their most intense expression in the cross" will still today need "helpful interpretation and restatement" (1955:159, 162).

In the concluding chapter Wilder again returns to a discussion of Bultmann who "offers us a concrete and masterly instance of the issues involved in dealing with the language of faith" (1955:179). However, once again and again correctly, he criticizes Bultmann because he "underlines the obsolete character of these symbols" (1955:176). It is not the symbols that are obsolete or dead but their hermeneutics that has faltered and failed. "Hosts of men today are alienated from the

Christian faith in part because orthodoxy has misused the language of faith" (1955:180).

2.5   Theology and Literature

In November of 1956 Wilder gave the five William Belden Noble Lectures in the Harvard University Memorial Church. These were later published as the five chapters of *Theology and Modern Literature* (1958c), and this book continues the literary pole of the dialectic under consideration in this chapter. In the years between this work and his last book of literary criticism (1952) Wilder's interests in theology and literature had been encouraged by two challenges. Towards the end of his time at Chicago, just prior to his 1954 move to Harvard, Reinhold Neibuhr invited Wilder to joint the editorial board of *Christianity and Crisis*, a position he held until after his retirement from Harvard in the middle sixties. Between 1952 and 1956 he wrote several editorials for the magazine but, if it is possible to infer from their declining annual numbers, Wilder must have preferred articles to editorials; and it was those former writings that he continued to publish for the periodical between 1956 and 1963. The other influence in that period prior to Harvard came from the emerging program of Marvin Halverson in the Department of Worship and the Arts of the National Council of Churches. He had been Dean of Students at the Chicago Theological Seminary in the forties; and when he organized committees on the various arts, Wilder was asked to join the Committee on Literature, a group which also "included W.H. Auden, Cleanth Brooks, the editors of the *Yale* and *Sewanee* reviews, the novelist Frederick Buechner, and others" (1958c:45). Work done under both these influences reappeared in the Noble lectures, with an article on "Artist and Believer" from *Christianity and Crisis* (1953c) subsumed into the first lecture (1958c: 4–10), and a draft statement prepared for the Committee on Literature, which also passed through *Christianity and Crisis* (1957a), transmuted into the second lecture (1958c:vii, 46–60).

In 1957 Wilder wrote an article for *The Christian Scholar* entitled "Christianity and the Arts" with the subtitle, "The Historic Divorce and the Contemporary Situation" (1957b). This subtitle summarizes the first three chapters or lectures in the Noble series. In the first one Wilder moved from literature towards theology, moved towards religion "from the side of the artist and critic" (1958c:39). In the second one the direction was reversed: "What bridges are being thrown out over the gulf from the side of the church?" (1958c:39). And the third chapter probed the challenge of "Christian discrimination," from the fathers to the moderns, and with special awareness that such "a program of Christian discrimination labors against the suspicion that a partisan, a dogmatic motive may be at work" (1958c:81).

The rest of the book is taken up with detailed applications of these general comments to a poet and a novelist, both of which chapters were later anthologized elsewhere (1958d, 1971b). "Poetry" was the term which appeared in the titles of Wilder's preceding books of criticism (1940a, 1952) but "Literature" was used in this one (1958c), and with that change greater emphasis on modern narrative starts to appear in Wilder's literary criticism.

The fourth chapter is "an examination of one modern literary presentation of Christ, that of the poet Robinson Jeffers in his poetic drama, *Dear Judas*" and its thesis "that Christ's empire over the hearts of men through the centuries rests upon the sheer fascination of agony and upon man's thinly veiled obsession with cruelty" (1958c:95, 96). This same theme is found in the poetry of Yeats, not only in "The Second Coming" but also in "Two Songs from a Play," and the section beginning, "Odour of blood when Christ was slain," is quoted by Wilder in this chapter's epigraph (1958c:92, 103). It could also be noted that Robert Frost has countered Yeats' charge in his own poem, *A Masque of Mercy*, with its laconic comment that violence had "been a commonplace/ Ever since Alexander Greeced the world" and its counter-suggestion that what Christ introduced was "a break with logic/ That made all other outrage seem a child's play." But the accusation that the centrality of the crucifixion had "exerted its power by an appeal to, and indeed a secret stimulus to, man's hidden obsession with suffering and even blood-lust" (1958c:104) comes not only from such poets as Jeffers or Yeats or Elder Olson ("the hanged staring Man") but also from writers such as Bernard Shaw. In Jeffers' poem, however, Jesus himself is quite well aware "that the power over mankind which will be his, will be achieved through suffering, and men's secret affinity for cruelty" (1958c:105). Wilder recognizes that the Cross can "easily pass over into forms that are more than suspect, as is evident in other aspects of Spanish Catholicism and especially in Latin America" (1958c: 108); but his response is that the gospels themselves give little support to such fascinations. "They portray a divine transaction whose import far transcends the feelings of a protagonist or the sensibilities of the observer. What is important for the Evangelists is the revelation mediated — the operation of God in the event — not the poignancies of the occasion" (1958c:109).

Turning, finally, to the modern novel, Wilder notes that the "novelist dealing with authoritarian societies, Puritan or feudal or totalitarian, can have a field day in combing out the strands of evil which blight the family and the individual, the noxious legacies which represent fate for every new generation" (1958c:114). In particular, "Faulkner's work certainly illustrates the demand made upon Christians, that they re-examine their moralities at least once in a millenium" (1958c:114–15). He focuses his attention on the *The Sound and the Fury* and how Faulkner discloses therein the "obsessive vestigial codes and rigidities . . . fossilized religous sanctions, conceptions, or rituals" (1958c:125) which effect "the decline and fall of the Compson family—a rotting family in a rotting house—all representative of a wider cultural fatality" (1958c:119). But with them he contrasts the black servant, Dilsey, in whom Christianity appears in its uncorrupted perennial and paradoxical theme of the power of grace in unexpected places, unexpected persons, and unexpected professions. "We learn how to recognize the incognitos of God" (1958c:131).

2.6   Gospel and Rhetoric

The final book to be considered balances the preceding literary one with an expected biblical complement, but it also brings more closely together the twin areas of bible and literature whose intercalation have structured this chapter.

In March of 1962 Wilder gave the Haskell Lectures at the Graduate School of Theology in Oberlin College, and many of the dominant themes of these lectures appeared in a short article he wrote for the Cullmann *Festschrift* around that same time (1962b). The lectures were later published, with an added seventh chapter on "Image, Symbol, Myth," in America as *The Language of the Gospel: Early Christian Rhetoric* and in England with title and subtitle reversed. It was this latter sequence that was used in the 1971 reissue of the volume and for this republication Wilder added a new introduction (1971b:xi–xxx). The volume was dedicated "To Colleagues and Students in the Harvard Divinity School, 1954–1963." This combination of Oberlin and Harvard appropriately connected Wilder's first two years of college, at Oberlin in 1913–1915, with his retirement from Harvard in 1963. He mentioned the "special pleasure" afforded him by this "return to Oberlin" (1971b: ix) and, elsewhere, he has underlined how "significant to me as one concerned with the issues of pacifism and the moral aspects of the war was my experience as a student at Oberlin College in 1914–15. President Henry Churchill King in his large Sunday Bible class dealt for many months with the origins of the war, with an analysis of Prussianism, traditional views of church and state, and the Christian attitude to war. The upshot was in effect a justification of American participation with the Allies . . . King, like myself, was a Congregationalist and with Oberlin as a whole represented the tradition of the abolitionists and of the New England theocrats, according to which the church associates itself with the moral responsibility of the state" (1968a:346).

Wilder's return to Oberlin had also far more ancient resonances. He had been born on September 18, 1895, as the oldest child (Thornton, 1897; Charlotte, 1898; Isabel, 1900; Janet, 1910) of Isabella Niven and Amos Parker Wilder. His mother's grandfather was Arthur Tappan who had been prominent in the founding of Oberlin College. And his father had been brought up as a Congregationalist, a tradition still strong at Oberlin when Amos and Thornton went there for two years before continuing on to Yale University.

Wilder's Oberlin lectures were concerned "not so much with what the early Christians said as how they said it. Yet this is a false distinction. The two cannot really be separated, but they can be looked at separately" (1971b:2). This purpose involves a focus on language. Wilder notes that "any human language represents a special kind of order superimposed upon existence. Generations live in it as a habitat in which they are born and die. Outside it is nescience" (1971b:5). And language was of paramount importance for both Judaism and Christianity. "Of course, like all religions Christianity has its sacred actions and spectacles, sacred places and times, sacred arts and objects, but it is in connection with God speaking that they are sacred" (1971b:11). At this point Wilder initiates an emphasis on oral over scribal language, on speaking over writing, which will have implications throughout his entire book. "Even the writing forms of the Early Church are better understood if we keep in mind the primal role of oral speech in the beginning. *Viva voce* communication is more malleable, more personal and more searching. These qualities were to distinguish Christian discourse even when it was obliged to take on written form" (1971b:13). There are, however, serious questions which could be raised against the chronological primacy of orality becoming a theological primacy without more detailed discussion and debate. Is there, for example, any more freedom in oral speech's openness to different iterations than in written speech's openness to different interpretations? And might one not argue, for example, that one can encounter the divine as well or even better in the absence of the writer than in the presence of the speaker? Or, finally, is it wise to *write* about the primacy of orality and to cite the scripted Scriptures in one's favor? In any case, as Wilder later notes, "roughly seven-tenths of the New Testament is anonymous or pseudonymous" (1971b:32), and that is presumably a gain not available in oral discourse.

Wilder places special emphasis on two features of "the new utterance" of primitive Christianity and both bespeak the depth of language and of world that was invoked in that experience. The first feature is *vernacularity*. There was little evidence of sacred or mantic or esoteric speech, "there was no flight from the vernacular" (1971b:18). A second feature was *brevity*. "At least we can say that it was not diffuse or verbose" (1971b:21). Both features together indicate that we are dealing with "revelation, not persuasion" (1971b:21) and that this is to be explained in the ordinariness of everyday existence.

In turning to the specific studies which follow on these general remarks, Wilder reiterates that "oral speech is where it all began"

(1971b:40), which is quite true, and then qualifies this by commenting "that the fundamental matter is not the distinction between oral and written, but between personal and impersonal, between first-hand and second-hand" (1971b:43), and that is both equally true and much more important. Still, his search is "to uncover the older deposits of early Christian speech behind the New Testament writings" (1971b:42). And these deposits appear in three major forms: dialogue, story, poem (1971b:42–43).

Dialogue, Wilder maintains, is "an inevitable form of rhetorical expression" within the Bible since "God is known as one who speaks, addresses, calls, initiates agreements or covenants, engages in public trial-scenes" (1971b:44). Wilder exemplifies this from the direct dialogue within several of Jesus' parables to the *diatribe* style within many of Paul's letters, and he draws particular attention, as did Auerbach's *Mimesis*, to the direct dialogue between Peter and the maid during the trial of Jesus in Mark 14 (1971b:48). Wilder recognizes quite fully the fateful nature of such a "plebeian, low-life episode involving personages that are nonentities" (1971b:48), but he draws no attention to the differences between a dialogue in which God (through prophet or some other human intermediary) directly addresses the hearer and a dialogue such as that in Jesus' parables or in Mark's trial episode where God is not a speaker, yet the horizontal human dialogue is transversed by a vertical transcendental one in which God speaks by metonymic or metaphoric extension to all future hearers or readers. It must surely be important whether God speaks directly *in* a dialogue or indirectly *through* a dialogue. Wilder makes no distinction between these two forms of dialogue but holds them together noting that "we may find in the dialogue between heaven and earth that occurs in the New Testament elements of distortion, or hyperbole and incomprehension. We shall find an analogy to this in the traits of the extraordinary that Jesus introduces into the otherwise lifelike circumstances of his parables" (1971b:50).

Story is discussed by Wilder under two headings. There are first of all stories *about* Jesus such as the cure of blind Bartimaeus in Mark 10:46–52 (1971b:55–70) and then there are stories *by* Jesus, the parables (1971b: 71–88). Wilder grounds his consideration of story in the statement that "God is an active and purposeful God and his action with and for men has a beginning, a middle and an end like any good story" (1971b:56). This means that Christians are located "in the very midst of the great story and plot of all time and space, and therefore relate us to the great dramatist and storyteller, God himself" (1971b: 57). It is not clear how literally Wilder wishes all this to be taken. On the one hand, he talks of this "total story of Paradise Lost and Paradise Regained" (1971b:60) so that one could, though he does not, raise the issue of *the genre of the canon*, the mode of this total biblical story so plotted by God. On the other hand, "that which makes the peculiar mystery of the life of the Christian is that the world plot plays itself over in him, yet in such a way that it is always unprecedented" (1971b:58). A total plot of which the individual units and particular incidents are metonyms of the whole is a very special form of narrative. Somewhere between these two modes of story, then, one would have to understand Wilder's claim that "with this kind of a God the story was the proper kind of witness even more than the saying or the dialogue" (1971b:69).

In underlining the everyday normalcy and even "secularity" (1971b:73) of Jesus' parables, Wilder understands that "Jesus, without saying so, by his very way of presenting man, shows that for him man's destiny is at stake in his ordinary creaturely existence, domestic, economic and social" (1971b:74). There is then one sentence where Wilder is on the brink of asking himself a crucial question derived from this understanding but from which he quickly moves away. "We cannot but be surprised by the fact that such incomparable human and naturalistic and artistic portrayal of human life should come to us from one who spoke out of an acute eschatological crisis" (1971b:77). Had that surprise been pursued Wilder would have had to distinguish between different modes of eschatological vision in order to locate Jesus' understanding more precisely among them. Magnificent poetry may well derive from an apocalyptic or gnostic eschatology, but what type of eschatology is profoundly at home in realistic everyday normalcy and detailed secular description? In this one instance Wilder's own rhetoric obscures the crucial issue. "Some are tempted, therefore, to say that the Jesus of the parables alone is the real Jesus, and that the fanciful and perfervid sayings of an apocalyptic kind cannot be authentic. The Jesus of the parables is sane; the Jesus who speaks of the Son of Man coming with the clouds is fanatical. The Jesus of the parables is a true humanist; the eschatological Jesus is a cloudy visionary" (1971b:80). Even those for whom the apocalyptic imagination would never be described in such prejudicial terms as fanciful, perfervid, fanatical, cloudy—for whom, indeed, it is one of the magnificent options of the human imagination *in extremis*—may still want to ask three very basic questions. Do the Son of Man sayings derive originally from the historical Jesus? And, if they do not, what mode of eschatological vision best explains the parables and aphorisms, miracles, and conflicts of this Jesus? Finally, is there such a thing as anti-apocalyptic eschatology and is that where Jesus might best be located? These questions indicate that Wilder has still not pressed the problem of the relationship between mystical and apocalyptic eschatology which he had first noted in the forties and which was seen in #1.3 above (1941a, 1978a:194–214).

The poem in "the New Testament is based on two different traditions, that of Hellenistic paganism and that of Israel" (1971b:92). The tradition of Israel reappeared in the New Testament and, in terms of these origins, one can distinguish: "(1) the 'gnome': the aphorism of the wisdom tradition of Israel, often found in highly patterned and pungent form; (2) the 'oracle': inspired by rhythmic warning, promise, vision, curse, in the tradition of Old Testament prophecy; (3) the 'psalm': liturgical prayer-poems in the tradition of the psalter" (1971b: 92–93). Apart from these sources, however, there are also cases such as that of the poem in Col 1:15–20 where a "pagan mythological poem has been converted into a Christian baptismal confession" (1971b:111–12). Wilder concludes by observing that we who have learned poetry from a Rilke or a Yeats or a Wallace Stevens may find the New Testament poetry too simple, naive, or primitive for our tastes. But "the poetry of the New Testament, with some exceptions, can best be seen as the voice not of an established culture and sensibility, but of an iconoclastic moment and crisis in culture. Primitive Christian poetry is spoken, as it were, at the beginning of a world, indeed, at the beginning of the world" (1971b:116). It is no small experience ever to have glimpsed such an hour and ever to have heard its voice.

As mentioned earlier, when the Oberlin lectures were first published in 1964, Wilder added a final chapter on "one aspect of the new speech that we have so far recognized only in an indirect way, that is its metaphorical and symbolic character" (1971b:118). His thesis is that "the Gospel arose out of that kind of radical break in human affairs when old customs and continuities are undermined; it reflected that level of experience in which man and the world are made and unmade, and in which language will inevitably have a dynamic character and inevitably take on symbolic or surreal expression" (1971b:123). This thesis appeared in another article from the same time which claimed that "in the rise of the Gospel we have a language-event . . . in which a seismic disturbance overtook existing rhetorics whether Jewish or Hellenistic" (1964b:25). The negative implications of this are spelled out quite clearly: "If then we appreciate rightly the plastic and mythological character of much of the New Testament, we are not tempted to literalize it" (1971b:124). And the result of this inability to literalize must be, now as then, a certain interpretive diversity. In other places Wilder has drawn specific attention to parallels between debates in the Johannine churches of the New Testament and contemporary Baptist churches in the Baltic States (1957c:210, 1961c:418–19). Yet he is far less sympathetic to contemporary reformulations of that seismic or eschatological *moment* wherein the Gospel arrived. "Existentialist hermeneutic as· we see it today, rightly challenging, as it does, biblicism, historicism, and theological positivism, is nevertheless in danger of setting up a nonhistorical kerygmatic absolute" (1962c:50). Or again: "The new hermeneutic rests on a violent acultural and anticultural impulse and sees both the divine word and the human response in a kind of cultural vacuum" (1964a:204). But such accusations might have been as easily made against early Christian rhetoric in its own inaugural moment from within the pieties of those who spoke without it. It is quite true, necessarily true, to hold that "the actual language continuities of Christianity with its antecedents certainly limits the terms in which we can use absolutes or paradox about the new event of the Gospel" (1964b:24). But in seismic event or eschatological language continuities are usually much more visible afterwards, maybe long afterward, when the earthquake is over and rebuilding can begin.

CHAPTER 3
IMAGINATION AND RELIGION

My experience in WWI initiated me into dimensions of the imagination which have made much of life and letters seem insipid by comparison, but which confirmed for me the authority of the classics, and above all, the Scriptures. Any who read the poems in my first book of verse, *Battle-Retrospect*, published in the Yale Series of Younger Poets, may well be scandalized by the nostalgia there expressed. They should recognize that the drama of taking part in world-shaping events has its own repercussions. In any case, imagining the real could never thereafter be satisfied with what most modern classics or iconoclasts could view as important.

(1978b:33–34)

My war experience and my life experience have seemed to teach me some priorities. One of these is that salvation has to be political; it is not enough for the soul to be enlightened. Another is that liberation and emancipation are not enough, as we envisage them. There is a deeper liberation called for which costs a great deal more.

(1978b:56)

Amos Wilder joined the Divinity School of Harvard University "in the fall of 1954 after Henry Cadbury's retirement" (1961d:11). Cadbury had succeeded James Hardy Ropes in 1934 "as Hollis Professor of Divinity, a chair founded in 1721 and therefore the oldest endowed chair in any field in the United States" (1975c:315). Wilder himself received this professorship in 1955, and when he retired from Harvard in 1963, it was as Hollis Professor of Divinity, Emeritus. His decade of teaching there had seen not only the "intensity, if not virulence, of the debate" over the university's Memorial Church (1958e:13), but, more importantly, it had coincided with "a time when the growth in enroll-ment of the school became marked" (1961d:11). To that expansion Wilder brought an experience in theological education both chronologi-cally and geographically diverse. He had his own immediate knowledge of Montaubon, France, in 1919, the University of Brussels in 1920–21, and Oxford University in 1921–1923, as well as of the University of Frankfurt in 1951–1953, when he delivered the Convocation Address at the Harvard Divinity School, September 19, 1954, on "Theological Education Abroad: Discussions in England, France, and Germany" (1954d).

After his official retirement from teaching, Wilder's writings con-tinued to probe that same dialectic of contemporary literature and biblical tradition which is now discussed at that deeper level where the polarities of the debate are best expressed as imagination and religion. First, however, there is an even more important aspect of Wilder's work to be considered.

3.1   Ecumenism and Scholarship

In reading over Wilder's reviews, for example in *The Chicago Theological Seminary Register* during the years he was teaching there (1943–1954), or his editorials and articles in *Christianity and Crisis* (1952–1965) from the time Reinhold Niebuhr brought him on its Editorial Board, as well as his essays and books over fifty years of publication, one is particularly struck by his consistent ability to disagree without disrespect, to characterize without caricature, and to debate without debasing his opponent, his subject, or himself.

This graceful gift for irenic debate is very evident in three articles Wilder published in the sixties after his retirement from Harvard.

The first article was generated by the Ecumenical Institute of Bossey, Switzerland, which held a "Consultation for New Testament Scholars on the Ecumenical Perspectives of Their Work" at Montreal, July 26 to August 1, 1963, under the direction of Erich Dinkler of Heidelberg. Wilder asks this question: "In the existing churches and sects, in their articles of belief, catechisms, doctrines, interpretations, we face a chaos of cumulative and conflicting partialities, over-interpretations, omissions, though it can also be said that they all are in selective ways pointers to the original text and revelation. But we have seen that such differences go back, finally, to differences in the formulations of the New Testament text itself. What criteria do we have by which we can go behind such differences to the Word-Action of God Himself?" (1965a:209). It is certainly no small step to acknowledge that later Christian pluralism after the New Testament period may well be the inevitable result of primitive Christian pluralism within the New Testament text, but this would render it unlikely that any formulation of this "Word-Action of God" would ever be acceptable to all Christians. Could it be that symbol unifies but that interpretation always and necessarily diversifies? And could it be that the only ultimate ecumenical unity is based on accepting the inevitability of such pluralism in interpretation within a unity of symbol?

The next two articles were not concerned with intra-Christian differences but with Jewish-Christian relationships. The more institutional aspects of this dialogue in the various assemblies and institutes of the World Council of Churches are surveyed by Wilder in the first article. He concludes that "there is only one temptation from the beginning, a temptation that underlies all others: not to think largely enough about the charity of God . . . . In the measure that the divine magnanimity is grasped, the underlying oneness of the People of God manifests itself, whether between church and church, or between Israel and Church" (1966:83). The other article is more concerned with the historical aspects of the dialogue in the New Testament, generally in Paul and particularly in Matthew. His thesis is that "the New Testament as a whole reflects this tension in depth before the final institutional separation, and documents the intra-Jewish controversy and polemic occasioned by the Gospel" (1968b:347). The most important result of reading the New Testament polemics in the light of this acceptance is an awareness that (1968b:356):

> Christian thinking about Christ and the Gospel has never been final but still draws upon the one heritage of the one People for fuller understanding. That is, it is incomplete without the continuing witness of Israel past and present. The mistake of the Church after the fluid intra muros period of the first century was to absolutize and harden its Christological formulations. By forgetting the proleptic character of the Gospel it has in various ways cut itself off from full solidarity with God's elective purpose and power. One clear indication of this is seen in the scandalous attitudes to the Jews which have so generally marred the history of the Church from the time of the Apostolic Fathers to the present.

3.2   Novelty and Continuity

The Society for the Arts, Religion and Contemporary Culture, founded in 1961, sponsors an annual Paul Tillich Commemorative Lectureship in honor of that distinguished founding Fellow. In 1968 Amos Wilder delivered those lectures at New Harmony, Indiana, the site of Tillich's burial, under the general title of "Modern Reality and the Renewal of the Word." This represented "an extensive recasting and supplementation of lectures given at Yale University in 1956 under the auspices of the William Lyon Phelps Lectureship" (1969a:13). For publication purposes Wilder framed these three lectures with six other articles, some of which had already appeared in print during the preceding decade. This book, *The New Voice*, is subtitled "Religion, Literature, Hermeneutics," and thus continues Wilder's more recent emphasis on literature rather than poetry alone. The triadic subtitle also elevates "Hermeneutics" to a very important position in relation to both religion and literature.

The book is dedicated "To the Society for the Arts, Religion and Contemporary Culture and its Founder and First Director, Marvin P. Halverson, 1913–1967." This homage recalls Wilder's long association with Halverson from his days at Chicago Theological Seminary through his work as "Executive Director of the Department of Worship and the Arts of the National Council of Churches, 1952–1962, and later as Director of the Society" (1969a:13; see also 1976:43–46).

The book explores "the language crisis of our time . . . language here in the widest sense of all the vehicles of meaning and communication" (1969a:13–14) and discusses this situation with an introduction and three parts.

The introductory article is a theoretical statement concerning "theological criticism" (1969a:19–38) which had appeared earlier that same year in *Soundings* and was reprinted later in *Literature and Religion* (1969b). His own position is stated quite clearly at the outset. Put positively: "Though there is properly only one kind of criticism, only one cumulative discipline of criticism, yet contributions to it can be and have been made from various perspectives" (1969a:21). Put negatively: "I reject the idea of a specifically Christian criticism whether in terms of the experience of the believer or of theological categories" (1969a:21). The academic and institutional background of this position is the present situation where many religious scholars find "their base of operations is often now in the college and the university rather than in the seminary, and in departments in the humanities rather than of those in religion" (1969a:23). The social and cultural background supplies those conditions which "tend to relativize critical orthodoxies, to require interdisciplinary resources, and to open the interpretation of the arts of language to a total anthropological and linguistic approach" (1969a:23). When one has made all the cautions demanded, and disciplined one's presuppositions as closely as possible, the heart of the matter is still this: "The judge may not leap directly from Magna Carta or the Bill of Rights to the matter at hand. The moral theologian should not leap directly from the Sermon on the Mount to the present ethical decision. So also in the field of letters there is no shortcut for the believer" (1969a:25). Thus the core question: "How does such a critic move properly and convincingly from his faith to his literary judgments?" (1969a:26). It is not at all clear that Wilder answers this question in the rest of the chapter. Many of its general statements and specific examples seem eminently sensible, for example, its warnings against taking the new and the iconoclastic, the avant-garde and the contemporary with either too little or too much reverence and seriousness. Yet it is probably not enough to follow that core question just cited with this: "I do not, indeed, accept that view which insists upon the total incommensurability of divine and human things" (1969a:26). Since such a view would breach the very *totality* it claimed, that paradox might have been a good place to focus the problem of *theo*logical criticism, that is, a criticism which confronts precisely the divine and the human. What, in other words, if theological criticism begins not by criticizing literature theologically but by criticizing criticism theologically?

Part One of the book, "Biblical Genres and Archetypes," includes three sections: the first on narrative in the Old Testament, the next on Marcel Proust's masterpiece in particular, and the third on symbolism in the New Testament. This last section is a revised version of a paper prepared for a symposium on *Myth and Dream* sponsored by the Society for the Arts, Religion and Contemporary Culture (1970b). Wilder emphasizes three aspects of Old Testament epic against which to contrast the contemporary narrative. A first aspect is that "the narrative of the Bible takes time and its events seriously and above all provides a world-plot with a beginning, middle and end" (1969a:45). A second one is the "very rich dense portrayal of human experience" (1969a:61). And a third element is a certain stylistic tension so that "while in one dimension experience is ordered in teleological succession its reality is also evoked in another dimension which we may call the dialogical" (1969a:67). This third aspect is in some tension with the first one, but Wilder does not pursue this point. His judgment is that, against this biblical background, "we find the modern novel lacking in this kind of holism or total humanism" (1969a:75). A case in point is the lack in "holism of Proust's narrative" (1969a:87), *A la recherche du temps perdu*, where, Wilder judges, "our modern situation denied him more total apperceptions" (1969a:97). For example: "Except for his attention to the Dreyfus case his dealings with political and economic realities are conventional if not naive, and this lacuna inevitably limits the portrayal even of those circles and individuals he knows best" (1969a:87).

There are, however, certain weaknesses to this judgment and they are basic enough to the book's entire project to be noted immediately. First, Wilder had begun "by asking what might be called the prior question about narrative in general. What special aspect of our human reality discloses itself in the universal impulse to tell stories? . . . a story posits a sense of orientation and coherence. The story, the fable, the myth assume a context, an order of some kind. They impose a graph upon chaos or nescience. They carve out a lighted space, a *zu-Hause*, in the darkness" (1969a:56). We cannot live without such graphs, such spaces, and such homes. We can, unfortunately, deny that *we* imposed, carved, or built them. We can claim as author, destiny, history, nature or divinity. It is presumably equally inhuman to deny either their relativity or their necessity, but have we not surely learned by now that the relativity applies to their substance while the necessity applies to their structure? The relativity is of *this* graph or *that* graph but the necessity is of *some* graph or *any* graph. Intuitions of this dilemma may well explain the tension between teleological and dialogical aspects of biblical narrative. And certainly it is overt awareness of it that has so much modern narrativity less interested in graphs, spaces, and homes, than in the processes of imposing, carving, and building. In other words, a work that seeks to embrace all the perceptions humans have and another that seeks only to touch the nature of perception itself may both be equally, if differently, *total*. Second, is it fair to compare the Bible, as the edited and reedited, written and rewritten result of between one and two thousand years of cumulative vision, with *any* individual work of literature? Surely, and necessarily, any individual work will be deficient against such a whole even if some hold up better than others. On the other hand, if one were to focus on specific books or parts of the Bible would they not be just as partial and naive? Is, for example, Romans 13 any less "conventional if not naive" than Proust on "political and economic realities" (1969a:87). And finally, is it not precisely this type of expecting everything from everyone which Wilder deprecates in Robert Lowell's "understandable revulsion at what he took to be the two most immoral books in the Bible, Joshua and the Apocalypse" (1969a:59, n. 15).

The final article in the book's Part One concerns the "symbolics" of the New Testament, meaning "the social-psychological dimension of the symbol and the whole domain of cultural dynamics" (1969a:100). The focus of this chapter from the late sixties harks back to Wilder's doctoral dissertation from the early thirties. In discussing Jesus and the Pharisees Wilder emphasizes two warnings which should be carved in stone for any scholar who touches this subject. First, "the revolution in images initiated by Jesus should not be viewed as a war of myths between Judaism and Christianity. The divergence then as to this day is within the same household of faith" (1969a:118). Second, the pejorative connotations which Pharisaism has obtained from the bitter if somewhat contradictory accusations in the New Testament (legalistic *and* hypocritical?) cannot stand against this: "The Pharisees carried through their admirable ethico-juristic and casuistic program enriched by the haggada, and the ethics of the people was the loftiest in the world of that time with its emphasis on freedom and responsibility" (1969a:121–22). What then was at issue between Jesus and the Pharisees? In terms of eschatology Wilder has not moved much from his dissertation position. "The focal image of Jesus' message was that of the Kingdom of God viewed as imminent and constituting both grace and total demand. It is not enough to say that Jesus goes back to the prophets. The ultimate reference of his message and vision is that of the creation itself. This is suggested by the cosmic-eschatological character of the Kingdom which he announced, in this respect different from the eschatology of the Pharisees associated with the age to come and the national hope. It partakes of the total Alpha-Omega scope of apocalyptic without its curiosities and phantasmagoria" (1969a:116–17). This is not very satisfactory, especially since in so many other places Wilder himself has brilliantly defended those "curiosities and phantasmagoria" of the apocalyptic visions as being the inevitable products of imagination *in extremis* (1964b, 1971a). In terms of ethics, however, a far more profound distinction beings to appear. It is hardly more than hinted at through references to Paul Ricoeur's writings, especially in his *The Symbolism of Evil* (pp. 118–50). Ricoeur "asks whether the spiritual regime of the Law espoused by the Jewish teachers 'could recognize its own abysses'" (1969a:122). Thus "it is suggested that the imagery of Jesus represented in part a recovery of older archetypes, especially of those evoking the 'non-ethical face of evil,' thus demoralizing the patterns of his day" (1969a:122). When the ethics of Jesus are located at this level of depth and danger, the eschatology of Jesus will have to be relocated to that profundity as well. What Wilder has placed demurely in a "Note" at the end of this chapter (1969a:120–22) would require a complete rethinking of eschatology and ethics in the teaching of Jesus.

It is in the book's Part Two, "Vicissitudes of the Word in Our Time," however, that the subject of *The New Voice* receives its most direct discussion. Wilder himself proposes no theoretical analysis of the situation of modernity let along post-modernity. "We do not propose here to assess all the familiar analyses of modern alienation, secularization, dehumanization, desacralization, the breakup of the Christian synthesis, the dissociation of sensibility, the death of tragedy, and indeed, the death of God" (1969a:135). Nevertheless, if the *why* of the situation is not analyzed, the *what* is stated quite clearly. "In all the arts today we find that one of the recurring strategies is to go behind all existing patterns and to begin over with the first elements of language, at the very zero point of experience" (1969a:149). This zero point is obviously a very dangerous place to be since from it comes not only mysticism, apocalypticism, or gnosticism, but also nihilism, that "total denigration, inspired by diffused resentments or morbid world-loathing" (1969a:147). This zero point of experience, "as though man were to begin again at the ultimate roots of his being" (1969a:158), although clearly stated is not the primary focus of Wilder's interest in these three chapters. It is more the necessary interplay between novelty and continuity, creation and tradition, that is his central concern. This is exemplified in poetry such as Eliot's *Four Quartets* or Jones' *The Anathémata* where the archetypes of the past are overtly present in the subject matter. This hardly pays sufficient attention to other cases where the continuities are more silent and profound, where indeed the continuity is in the permanent discontinuities at the core of language and of narrative, where, finally, the major continuity is those traces of the "zero point" in the old as in the new and which we no longer recognize in the old because we have grown used to its initial shock. One of the most interesting features in these chapters is Wilder's conviction that we are in a period of "gestation" or "transition" (1969a:176, 177). He never even mentions the possibility that this period may be no more gestational or transitional than any other one. And this question goes to the very heart of Wilder's hermeneutics. What if the great discontinuities, fissures, and negativities of our period are not the passing prelude to new over-arching certainties but are the *via negativa* of our transcendence, so that we presently need not greater positive certainty but greater negative capability?

Part Three, the book's final section, is "Secular Repossession" and it brings together three articles of Wilder's spanning the preceding ten years (1959, 1962e, 1965b). These units, which include his Ingersoll Lecture on the Immortality of Man at Harvard University, are primarily concerned with the revelations and epiphanies found in contemporary art and literature rather than in the more traditional ecclesiastical and theological locations.

3.3 Theology and Theopoetic

Four of the six chapters in Wilder's book on *Theopoetic: Theology and the Religious Imagination* (1976) had already been published in the early seventies. Apart from Chapter 3, "Contemporary Mythologies and Theological Renewal" (1970c), the heart of the volume in Chapters 1, 4, and 5 had appeared as "Theology and Theopoetic" in *The Christian Century* (1973–74). "I believe that I had picked up the terms 'theopoetic' and 'theopoesis' from Stanley Romaine Hopper and his students, no doubt in one or another of the remarkable consultations on hermeneutics and language which he had organized at Drew and Syracuse" (1976:iv).

Wilder summarizes his thesis as a "plea for a theopoetic . . . doing more justice to the role of the symbolic and the prerational in the way we deal with experience . . . This plea therefore means according a greater role to the imagination in all respects of the religious life" (1976:2). Repeatedly throughout the volume he suggests that this war for the imagination must today be fought on two simultaneous fronts. "It must assert the rights of the imagination against abstraction, rationalism, and stereotype. But the enemy is also on the other side: the cult of the imagination for itself alone: vision, phantasy, ecstasy for their own sakes; creativity, spontaneity on their own, without roots, without tradition, without discipline" (1976:57). Again: "In a time like ours one must argue not only against those no-nonsense or cerebral types who identify the imagination with fancy. One must also awaken those who live an impoverished dream-life to the true dynamics of the spirit and to those impulses and poetries of the heart which orient us in the unknown" (1976:80). And, in final summation: "I have noted that a theopoetic or plea for a religious imagination has to defend itself on two fronts. It has to defend itself on the one hand against a pragmatic no-nonsense type of mentality, representing a kind of devastated area in a culture whose aesthetic and spiritual antennae have been blighted . . . . But today our plea has to defend itself on another front. In the current resurgence of spirituality, mysticism, and phantasy it is necessary to raise caveats and to call for discrimination. Here the critic appears himself to be opposed to creativity and liberation, and is put down as a traditionalist" (1976:101–102).

The three chapters of this book which derived from articles about theopoetic in *The Christian Century* explore respectively this theopoetic imagination (Chapter 1), and then defend it on the front of a too absolute rationalism (Chapter 4) and of a too facile mysticism (Chapter 5). But Wilder is obviously much more defensive on that second front than on the first one. It is clearly a far more difficult and dangerous one on which to fight. The book's sixth and final chapter, "Theopoetic and Mythopoetic," cites "Delmore Schwartz's poem 'Starlight like Intuition Pierced the Twelve,' published in the *Kenyon Review* in the summer of

1944" and comments that "what is remarkable here is to find the *total* thrust of the resurrection myth transmuted into the language of today in the work of a modern secular poet" (1976:96; my italics). One could agree completely with this assessment but still note that we are at least in the starlight and that the areas where the imagination is engaged on that second front are far, far darker than starlight or moonlight (as Delmore Schwartz also knew).

The book is framed by a series of *befores*. It opens with four of them, cited from Wilder's last book of poems, *Grace Confounding* (1972a), to which more detailed consideration will be given in the next section. "Before the message there must be the vision, before the sermon the hymn, before the prose the poem. Before any new theologies however secular and radical there must be a contemporary theopoetic. The structures of faith and confession have always rested on hierophanies and images. But in each new age and climate the theopoetic of the church is reshaped in inseparable relation to the general imagination of the time" (1976:1). The book concludes with two more of them. "Before oneiric and chthonic mysteries comes the waking life on earth. Before the moonlight world comes that of sunlight" (1976: 104). But what of a far more ancient wisdom that begins each day at sundown, that therefore has the night precede the day, and that therefore must say, from the very beginning of our story, "there was evening and there was morning, one day"?

3.4   Zero and Algebra

Under his father's early guidance Wilder spent most of his undergraduate summers either working on farms or studying at agricultural schools (1978b:10–11). He also spent the summer of 1920 in a Wall Street bank in New York City. It seems clear, however, that farming took and banking did not. It was nature rather than finance that was to be extolled in so many of his later poems. But in these poems it is constantly seen as the sounds and signs of divinity (1928:1):

> Rhythm is in the winds, and rhythm in the seas,
> The heavens chant in numbers, and the springtime and the fall
> Are pulses in the sagas of the gods, and centuries
> Are but the respiration of the eldest Bard of all.

And again (1928:22):

> Divine imagination ruled the scene:
> The transcendent artist, master of all form,
> Had woven together on the mountain screen
> The glooms of storm.

Whether as "eldest Bard" or "transcendent artist" or "eternal dreamer" (1928:22), this divinity appears primordially as "eternal mind" (1928: 9–10, 1943a:82):

> The spirit gropes
> In nameless visions and inhuman tracts
> Beyond earth's calms and storms,
> The eyeballs seared and blind
> With gazing on the eternal cataracts
> Of light that pour upon the world of forms
> From the exhaustless fountains of eternal mind.

(I resist resolutely the Celtic perversity that makes me wish to investigate more closely the phrase, "eternal cataracts," but I cannot resist mentioning the resistance.)

Yet the other side of divine mind seems often human pain (1923:12, 1943a:23):

> . . . Races of men, co-heirs of earth's duress,
> Children of night, and orphans of the void,
> Ringed 'round with menace and with mystery,
> Condemned at birth to death in loneliness
> Proscribed and hunted, trampled and destroyed
> By the blind furies of the earth and sea.

But, despite such "blind furies," or precisely because of them, Wilder can say (1928:51):

> And yet these strivings blind,
> This travail and this pain,
> Are tissue of some brain,
> The cell-work of a Mind
> That waxes as we wane.

Culture, on the other hand, more often raises darker problems for Wilder than does nature. In "*A Florentine Reverie*" on "The City of Man" (1923:59–60, 1943a:85, 87) one can look at:

> . . . the six bridges whose deep-shadowed spans
> Stir premonitions of obscurer worlds
> That lie beneath the piers of this we tread.

But, still, most of "the generations as they surge" will pass:

> In their small cosmos, and from birth to birth
> Without a glance turned on the aghast abyss
> Of thought, nor ever hearkening
> To the appalling roaring of the waters
> Risen in flood beneath the piers of day.

War, however, is not part of this dark side of culture. It seems almost part of nature in Wilder's poetry (1928:59):

I mourn no more the massacre
I mourn less for the million dead,
The soil from which the poppy springs
With fabulous decay is fed,
And from the dark's engulfed throng
Springs youth's immaculate new song.

Indeed, "to die was naught" (1928:49):

They died who came back to this blinder scene
And woke to know the solar year again,
Nor know the pit of souls and vast demesne
Of wars in heaven, but once again demean
Their lives to briefer cycles and contain
Their souls to briefer rounds and common pain . . . .

And this rhapsody for the fallen, "the enviable dead" (1923:36), recalls some earlier lines on the same trajectory (1923:9):

How are we fallen on another day
Whose life was a perpetual sacrament,
Supping with gods, and kneeling down to pray
In cataclysm when the world was rent,
As we strode shouting where the lightnings play!

One need not have attained the cold purity of pacifism to wonder if those lines speak more of paganism than of anything in either Jewish or Christian tradition.

The fundamental question to be asked of these poems, whether they are of nature or culture, of peace or of war, is this: Is all this human mind or Divine Mind? In a poem of 1924, which has appeared in three of Wilder's four volumes of poetry, he has said that "The signature of mind is on the deep" (1928:38, 1943a:58, 1972a:52). What happens as one begins to realize how much this signature of mind is human rather than divine? First, this happens (1928:78):

Men live in their imaginings, and weave
Terrors and tempests round them or deceive
Their souls with self-wrought curtains of despair,
And caught in their dark folds they perish there.
Fabrics of every hue these spirits spin,
And every tissue, and then live therein,
And some there be like mansions wrought of flame
But most are webs of torment and of shame.

And, then, this (1972a:39):

From so precarious, so absurd a station,
this foothold on make-believe,
it launches out,
fills its own space
with dizzy and endless exfoliations,
builds its own insubstantial architecture,
and leaving in oblivion that first fiction
inhabits its own adamantine order.

The more one considers this "first fiction," this "foothold on make-believe," the harder it may be to discern Divine Mind behind the screens of nature and culture. We may rather have to face a rupture of intelligibility. In a poem first published in *Poetry* (1965–66:168–69, 1972a:26–27) Wilder writes:

Death like a dam
arouses the deep;
off the Big Sur the shoals
surprise the currents of the main.
The hidden ledge
turns turquoise into snow,
and phosphorescence
burns round the granite reef.

Put more abstractly:

Accept no mitigation
but be instructed at the null point:
the zero
breeds new algebras.

This is later repeated with one minor change: "The null point/breeds new algebras." Wilder has come at last to a very dangerous vision since to be "instructed at the null point" must also mean to "be instructed by unreason." Throughout *all* his writings Amos Wilder has been consistently more interested in the new algebras than in the zero or null point but those reiterated lines lie as gages before the future and force it to ask what might such words entail. What does it mean to say, not that the old algebras breed the new ones as if in positive dialogue, but that the zero does, as if in negative dialectic? What does it mean that the zero is singular and the algebras, old or new, are plural? Is there a zero in all algebras, old and new, and is it only, or just especially, recognized in the transition from one to the other? Is it possible to grasp the new algebra and never know the zero, or know it, forget it, and then deny it? Is there an algebra, old or new, that permanently displays the zero that bore it? All these questions are dangerous and vertiginous and it is surely unsafe to linger too long at the null point, the zero, the instant of unreason. From thence must come not only mysticism, apocalypticism, gnosticism, but also nihilism, that fearful drive to make one's suicide as social as possible. One must certainly insist, as Wilder so eloquently has done, that both the zero and the algebra are necessary and that only in conjunction is either fully human. But by ignoring some safer line claiming that old algebras breed new ones, Wilder has made it possible to ask whether much of our western horror has arisen not from too much zero in our humanity but from too much algebra, especially where such algebra is mimetic of some more absolute algebra above, behind, before, or below it.

EPILOGUE
SEEDS AND FOUNDATIONS

What, then, of Wilder's influence on American biblical criticism? Of what type was it and could it have been quantitatively and qualitatively better or wider?

Wilder's chosen position has always been structural and relational rather than substantial and objectional (let the pun stand). He has chosen to stand between art and religion, between literature and theology. In a period when people believe in substances and objects, and hence in divided disciplines and divergent departments, such a position is doubly dangerous. Returning to the image of my title and my prologue, it takes a fragile craft to choose a fragile craft for one's academic salvation. As a period changes, however, and people come more to regard structures and relations than substances and objects, a location on an *and* may still be to stand on fragility but it may also be consummate craft. In writing this book I had to read Wilder's entire output of more than sixty years. What was most startling to me was how seldom I was bored. Throughout this review I have always kept in critical dialogue with Wilder's own work. I never found that I had to give decent burial and peaceful rest to opinions or discussions now long outdated. Wilder has been consistently capable of considering any subject at a depth where, even when that subject passes, the deep does not.

His own position in the academic between-world of the *and* was peculiarly appropriate in understanding the cosmic between-world of the apocalyptic imagination in first century Christianity as well as the cosmic non-world between premodernism and modernism in twentieth-century Christianity. My own personal conviction is that the contemporary situation of many of us is no longer between premodernism and modernism but between modernism and postmodernism. But here once again is that peculiarly fragile strength of Wilder's position. He was studying the *between,* be it in the early first or early twentieth centuries, and so his work is still fertile for considerations of another *between*, this time in the late twentieth century. Maybe, finally, one is always located on an *and* or living in a *between*.

But, one could object, were not other eminent biblical scholars equally involved in such an *and* or such a *between*: what of bible and archeology, for instance, or the bible and history? Why, then, is there no Wilder school of bible and literature just as there is an Albright school of bible and archeology? It is, however, precisely the point that such schools have never really given enough critical attention to that *and*, so this very weakness now makes their entire foundations insecure.

What is being approached here is, first, a distinction between founding one's work on the *and*, be it of bible *and* literature or bible *and* history, archeology, etc., as against founding one's work on the objects so related, thus oscillating from bible to literature or from bible to history, archeology, etc., without ever facing the theoretical problem of the *and*. And, second, there is the question of what type of influence derives respectively from those twin options. It seems necessary to suggest a distinction between seminal and fundamental influence, between influence as a seed and influence as a foundation. When we think about German biblical scholarship we think primarily of schools, of founding scholars, of theses directed, and thus of foundations. American biblical scholarship usually thinks of influence along the lines of these prodigious edifices which have so vastly enriched our field for so long. But Wilder has always seemed more at home in France ("Those of us for whom France has been our first love outside our own land" [1944a:528]) than in Germany; and France is the special home of seminal thinkers who do not so much found a school to direct as engender movements which they then struggle to disown. Wilder's influence is therefore far more difficult to assess since it operates seminally rather than foundationally. This is, of course, both its weakness and its strength; the foundation cracks but the seed endures, the heavy boat sinks to the bottom but the fragile craft is whirled up and clear of the whirlpool.

If it is granted that Wilder's influence on American biblical scholarship has operated seminally rather than foundationally, one must still ask about the quantity and quality of that influence. Was it as much and as good as it might have been? Wilder spoke, after all, from the oldest endowed chair in America and from one of America's greatest universities, so none of this was done in a corner.

It may well be that the very concept of seminal rather than foundational influence renders that question impossible to answer. Yet it seems also impossible not to ask it. Leaving aside, for here and now, what Wilder said to ecclesiastical concerns, he spoke primarily to two academic constituencies, to those involved either with biblical studies or with religion and literature. And the responses of these groups as organized and institutionalized entities can hardly be judged impressive. On the one hand, biblical studies, despite evident respect and specific honors, has been unbelievably slow in accepting, absorbing, and acting upon Wilder's basic challenge. Surely, slowly, steadily, but only in the seventies does it seem that the message is striking home. Philological and historical sophistication were always present in biblical studies and will always have to be present. But only now are items continually appearing which could be shown to colleagues in literature without undue embarrassment. It is still not clear whether biblical studies has grasped the full implications of Wilder's vision. This does not mean treating the Bible *as if* it were literature alone but rather asking what happens when religion and literature come together in the Bible. It involves learning the art of literary criticism not from reading other literary critics but from immersing oneself in literature itself. One could therefore fault, and to a lesser extent still fault, the institution of biblical studies for a very inadequate response to Wilder and for thus muting his influence, even his seminal influence, both quantitatively and qualitatively. I am also inclined to fault the institutionalized aspects of religion and literature as well, even though Wilder may have helped to create this arena. It seems almost as if biblical students stayed away from the literature aspects of Wilder's work while the religion and literature students stayed away from his biblical work. But Wilder has always stood on the *and* between religion and literature and has always pointed to the Bible as the place where the roots of our tradition arose as both together. It seems to me precisely on the Bible that this second constituency failed him. One might even ask, with a polemical edge not usually present in Wilder's irenic writings: Why are students of religion and literature afraid of the Bible? They seem more at home with biblical symbolism in literature than with biblical symbolism in the Bible itself. Once again, a second constituency ignored Wilder's specific and fundamental challenge, and it is not yet clear if they ever even heard it: What happens when religion and literature comes together *in the Bible* and at the roots of our tradition? My own judgment, then, is that Wilder's influence, even granted its seminal character, should have been quantitatively and qualitatively greater. The reason it was not was audience failure—a failure on the part of biblical studies which is now being belatedly redeemed and a failure on the part of religion and literature studies which still seems unredeemed. Indeed, it now seems that "secular" literary critics are becoming more interested in the Bible than are religion and literature students themselves.

There is a passage in 1 Cor 3:5–11 where Paul uses two metaphors, that of the seed and that of the foundation. One can almost see him decide to abandon the former and stay with the latter. "I planted, Apollos watered, but God gave the growth. So neither he who plants nor he who waters is anything, but only God who gives the growth. He who plants and he who waters are equal, and each shall receive his wages according to his labor. For we are God's fellow workers; you are God's field, [*and now the metaphor changes*] God's building. According to the grace of God given to me, like a skilled master builder I laid a foundation, and another man is building upon it. Let each man take care how he builds upon it. For no other foundation can any one lay than that which is laid, which is Jesus Christ."

I have suggested that Wilder's influence is more like that of a seed than that of a foundation. Even if Paul preferred the latter metaphor, we know that Jesus himself used the former one and talked of his own teaching as sowing rather than building and as organic rather than architectural. And John, if not Paul, was willing to accept the implications of Jesus' teaching for Jesus' own person: "Unless a grain of wheat falls into the earth and dies, it remains alone; but if it dies, it bears much fruit" (John 12:24). We know how profoundly Wilder has responded to the image of sowing, but it is also interesting and revealing to see the other metaphors he chooses in saying that "the basic paradigm of man's initiative vis-à-vis his world and its sequel could employ other types of venture: not only sowing but fishing, and also hunting, digging, mining, risking, investing, gambling" (1974b:141–42).

BIOGRAPHICAL OUTLINE

1895   Born September 18, in Madison, Wisconsin.

1900–1910   Early schooling in Madison (until 1906); Hongkong (six months); Berkeley, California.

1911–1913   Thacher School, Ojai, California.

1913–1915   Oberlin College (freshman, sophomore).

1915–1916   Yale University (junior).

1916–1919   War Service: American Ambulance Service (1916–1917); U.S. Field Artillery (1917–1919); studies at University of Toulouse and Montauban Seminary.

1919–1920   Yale University (senior). B.A.

1920–1921   University of Brussels.

1921–1923   Mansfield College, Oxford (theology: first and second year).

1923–1924   Yale Divinity School (third year). B.D.

1924–1925   Travel, including the Near East.

1925–1928   Minister of First Church of Christ (Congregational), North Conway, New Hampshire. Ordained minister, 1926.

1928–1930   Graduate study: Yale (1928–1929), Harvard (1929–1930). Yale Ph.D., 1933 (New Testament).

1930–1933   Associate Professor of Ethics and Christian Evidences, Hamilton College.

1933–1943   Norris Professor of New Testament, Andover Newton Theological School.

1935   Married Catharine Kerlin. Two children: Catharine Dix (31 Jan 1937) and Amos Tappan (6 Feb 1940).

1943–1954   Professor of New Testament, Chicago Theological Seminary and Federated Theological Faculty of the University of Chicago.

1954–1963   Hollis Professor of Divinity (since 1955), Harvard Divinity School.

Since 1963   Hollis Professor of Divinity, Emeritus.

WORKS CONSULTED
(Amos Niven Wilder)

1923   *Battle-Retrospect and Other Poems.* Yale Series of Younger Poets 16. New Haven, CT: Yale University Press. (Reprinted) New York: AMS, 1971.

1928   *Arachne: Poems.* New Haven, CT: Yale University Press.

1931   "The Nature of Jewish Eschatology." *JBL* 50: 201–6.

1932   "Marriage of Minors." *ChCent* 49: 735.

1933   *The Relation of Eschatology to Ethics in the Teaching of Jesus as Represented in Matthew.* Unpublished doctoral dissertation, Yale University.

1935   Review of William L. Sperry, *Wordsworth's Anti-Climax* (Cambridge, MA: Harvard University Press, 1935). *ChCent* 52: 1146–47.

1937a   "Historical and Transcendental Elements in Jesus' View of the Future." *JBR* 5: 117–19.

1937b   Review of C. John McCole, *Lucifer at Large* (London: Longmans, Green & Co., 1937). *ChCent* 54: 1359.

1940a   *The Spiritual Aspects of the New Poetry.* New York: Harper. (Reprinted; Freeport, NY: Books for Libraries Press, 1968).

1940b   "A Poet and the Class Struggle: Two Stages." *Poetry* 56: 32–39.

1940c   "Christian Significance of Recent Poetry." *Christendom* 5: 524–33.

1940d   Review of W.B. Yeats, *Last Poems and Plays* (New York: Macmillan, 1939). *ChCent* 57: 878.

1941a   "Jesus and the Charismatic Type." *JBR* 9: 151–54.

1941b   "Voices of Our Day." *Social Action* 7/5: 3–30.

1942a   "Christian Ethics and the Way of the Cross." *Crozer Quarterly* 19: 135–40.

1942b   "Democratic Culture in the Light of Modern Poetry." Pp. 358–73 in *Second Symposium of the Conference on*

Science, Philosophy and Religion. Ed. Lyman Bryson et al. New York: Harper.

1943a   *The Healing of the Waters: Poems.* New York: Harper.

1943b   "Don Quixote in the American Scene." *ATR* 25: 272–80.

1943c   "The Man Who Looked Like God: The Story of Armand Branche." *Motive* 4/1: 13–15.

1943d   "Variant Traditions of the Resurrection in Acts." *JBL* 62: 307–18.

1944a   Review of George Bernanos, *Plea for Liberty* (New York: Pantheon, 1944). *Christendom* 9: 528–30.

1944b   "Paul through Jewish Eyes." *JBR* 12: 181–87, 243.

1945   "Theology and Cultural Incoherence." *Approaches to National Unity: Fifth Symposium of the Conference on Science, Philosophy and Religion.* Ed. Lyman Bryson et al. New York: Harper.

1945–46   "Interpreting the Time." *Religion in Life* 15: 75–90.

1946a   "Equivalents of Natural Law in the Teaching of Jesus." *JR* 26: 125–35.

1946b   "The Revised New Testament: Pros and Cons." *The Atlantic Monthly* 178/6: 138–42.

1947a   "Literary Sources." Pp. 87–108 in *Foundations of Democracy.* Ed. Frederick Ernest Johnson. New York: Institute for Religious and Social Studies (Harper).

1947b   "New Testament Theology in Transition." Pp. 419–36 in *The Study of the Bible Today and Tomorrow.* Ed. Harold R. Willoughby. Chicago: University of Chicago Press.

1948a   "The Eschatology of Jesus in Recent Criticism and Interpretation." *JR* 28: 177–87.

1948b   "The Puritan Heritage in American Culture." *ThToday* 5/1: 22–38.

1948c   "Heilsgeschichte and the Bible." *Christendom* 13: 10–17.

1948d   "New Testament Faith and its Relevance Today." *The Shane Quarterly* 9: 63–129.

1950a   "Theology and Cultural Incoherence: A Restatement." Pp. 631–57 in *Perspectives on a Troubled Decade: Tenth Symposium of the Conference on Science, Philosophy and Religion.* Ed. Lyman Bryson et al. New York: Harper.

1950b   "Mythology and the New Testament," (essay review of
             Kerygma und Mythos; ed. H. Bartsch; Hamburg: Reich &
             Heidrich, 1948). *JBL* 69/2: 113–127.

1951a   "The Sermon on the Mount." Pp. 155–64 in *The Inter-
             preter's Bible*. Vol. 7. Ed. G. Buttrick. 12 vols. Nashville,
             TN: Abingdon.

1951b   "The Christian Hope: Its Meaning for Today." *Religion
             in Life* 21: 10–19.

1952   *Modern Poetry and the Christian Tradition: A Study in the
             Relation of Christianity to Culture*. New York: Scribner.

1953a   "Opening and Closing Doors in Germany." *ChCent* 70:
             738–40.

1953b   "Moral Aspects of German Recovery." *Religion in Life*
             22: 527–37.

1953c   "Artist and Believer." *ChCrisis* 13: 123–25.

1954a   "Biblical Hermeneutic and American Scholarship." Pp.
             24–32 in *Neutestamentliche Studien für Rudolf Bultmann
             zu seinem 70. Geburtstag*. Ed. Walther Eltester. BZNW
             21. Berlin: Töpelmann.

1954b   "Myth and Symbol in the New Testament." Pp. 127–47
             in *Symbols and Values: An Initial Study. Thirteenth Sym-
             posium of the Conference on Science, Philosophy and
             Religion*. Ed. Lyman Bryson et al. New York: Harper.

1954c   *Otherworldliness and the New Testament*. New York:
             Harper.

1954d   "Theological Education Abroad: Discussions in Eng-
             land, France and Germany." *Harvard Divinity School
             Bulletin* 20/1: 41–51.

1954e   "The New Society in the New Age." Pp. 111–23 in *The
             Biblical Doctrine of Man in Society*. Ed. George Ernest
             Wright. Ecumenical Biblical Studies 2. London: SCM.

1955   *New Testament Faith for Today*. New York: Harper.

1956a   "Scholars, Theologians and Ancient Rhetoric." SBL
             Presidential Address, 1955. *JBL* 75: 1–11.

1956b   "Kerygma, Eschatology and Social Ethics." Pp. 509–36
             in *The Background of the New Testament and its Eschatol-
             ogy: Studies in Honor of C. H. Dodd*. (Eds.) W. D.
             Davies and D. Daube. Cambridge: Cambridge Universi-
             ty Press. (Reprinted) *Kerygma, Eschatology and Social
             Ethics*. Facet Books: Social Ethics Series 12. Philadel-
             phia: Fortress Press, 1966.

1957a   "The Church's New Concern with the Arts." *ChCrisis*
           17: 12–14.

1957b   "Christianity and the Arts." *The Christian Scholar* 40:
           261–68.

1957c   "I, II, III John: Introduction and Exegesis." Pp. 209–
           313 in *The Interpreter's Bible*. Vol. 12. Ed. G. Buttrick.
           12 vols. Nashville, TN: Abingdon.

1958a   "The Basis of Christian Ethics in the New Testament."
           Journal of Religious Thought 15/2: 137–46.

1958b   "Eschatological Imagery and Earthly Circumstance."
           NTS 5: 229–45.

1958c   *Theology and Modern Literature*. Cambridge, MA: Har-
           vard University Press.

1958d   "The Cross: Social Trauma or Redemption." *Daedalus*
           87/3: 22–36. (Reprinted) Pp. 99–117 in *Symbolism in
           Religion and Literature*. Ed. Rollo May. New York:
           Braziller, 1960.

1958e   "Christianity and the Campus." *The New Republic*
           139/24: 13–16.

1959   "The Ante-Rooms of Faith: The Modern Novel and the
           Theologians." *The New Republic* 141/11: 16–18.

1961a   "Autumn Fires (Translated from Hölderlin)." Pp. 10–
           11 in *Festschrift zum 75. Geburtstag von Theodor Spira*.
           Eds. H. Viebrock and W. Erzgräber. Heidelberg: Carl
           Winter.

1961b   "Social Factors in Early Christian Eschatology." Pp.
           67–76 in *Early Christian Origins: Studies in Honor of
           Harold R. Willoughby*. Ed. Allen Wikgren. Chicago:
           Quadrangle Books.

1961c   "Eleutheria in the New Testament and Religious Liber-
           ty." *Ecumenical Review* 13: 409–20.

1961d   "New Testament Study in the Divinity School." *Har-
           vard Divinity School Bulletin* 25/2: 9–16.

1962a   "Albert Schweitzer and the New Testament in the
           Perspective of Today." Pp. 348–62 in *In Albert Schweit-
           zer's Realms: A Symposium*. Ed. Abraham Aaron Ro-
           back. Cambridge, MA: Sci-Art.

1962b   "Form-History and the Oldest Tradition." Pp. 3–13 in
           Neotestamentica et Patristica [Cullmann Festschrift]. Ed.
           W. Van Unnik. NovTSup 6. Leiden: Brill.

1962c   "New Testament Hermeneutics Today." Pp. 38–52 in *Current Issues in New Testament Interpretation: Essays in Honor of Otto A. Piper.* Eds. W. Klassen and G. Snyder. New York: Harper.

1962d   "The Modern Wrestle with the Negation." *ChCrisis* 21: 246–49.

1962e   "Art and Theological Meaning." *USQR* 18: 37–47. (Reprinted) Pp. 407–19 in *New Orpheus.* Ed. Nathan Scott. New York: Sheed & Ward.

1963   "The New Quest for the Historical Jesus." *ChCrisis* 22: 245–48.

1964a   "The Word as Address and the Word as Meaning." Pp. 198–218 in *The New Hermeneutic.* Eds. J. Robinson and J. Cobb. New York: Harper.

1964b   "Eschatology and the Speech-Modes of the Gospel." Pp. 19–30 in *Zeit und Geschichte: Dankesgabe an R. Bultmann zum 80. Geburtstag.* Ed. Erich Dinkler. Tübingen: Mohr-Siebeck.

1964c   Review of Norman Perrin, *The Kingdom of God in the Teaching of Jesus* (Philadelphia: Westminster, 1963), and Gösta Lundström, *The Kingdom of God in the Teaching of Jesus* (Richmond, VA: John Knox, 1963). *Int* 18: 199–204.

1965a   "Reconciliation—New Testament Scholarship and Confessional Differences. Parts I & II." *Int* 19: 203–17, 312–27.

1965b   "Mortality and Contemporary Literature." *HTR* 58: 1–20. (Reprinted) Pp. 17–44 in *The Modern Vision of Death.* Richmond, VA: John Knox, 1967.

1965–66   "A Hard Death." *Poetry* 107: 168–69.

1966   "The World Council of Churches and Judaism." Pp. 72–84 in *Judaism and the Christian Seminary Curriculum.* Eds. J. Bruce Long et al. Chicago: Loyola University Press.

1968a   "At the Nethermost Piers of History: World War I, A View from the Ranks. For Jules Deschamps." Pp. 344–57 in *Promise of Greatness: The War of 1914–1918.* Ed. George A. Panichas. New York: John Day.

1968b   "The Church and Israel in the Light of Election." Pp. 347–57 in *Studia Evangelica IV.* Papers presented to the

Third International Congress on New Testament Studies held at Christ Church, Oxford, 1965. Ed. F. L. Cross. TU 102. Berlin: Akademie Verlag.

1969a   *The New Voice: Religion, Literature, Hermeneutics.* New York: Herder & Herder.

1969b   "The Uses of a Theological Criticism." *Soundings* 52: 84–98. (Reprinted) Pp. 37–52 in *Literature and Religion.* Ed. Giles Gunn. London: SCM.

1970a   "Eschatology and Ethics in the Teaching of Jesus." Pp. 200–207 in *The Judeo-Christian Heritage.* Ed. William J. Courtenay. New York: Holt, Rinehart & Winston.

1970b   "Myth and Dream in Christian Scripture." Pp. 68–90 in *Myths, Dreams, and Religion.* Ed. Joseph Campbell. New York: Dutton.

1970c   "Contemporary Mythologies and Theological Renewals." *Journal of Religious Thoughts* 27/3: 5–12.

1971a   "The Rhetoric of Ancient and Modern Apocalyptic." *Int* 25: 436–53.

1971b   *The Language of the Gospel: Early Christian Rhetoric.* New York: Harper, 1964 [*Early Christian Rhetoric: The Language of the Gospel.* London: SCM, 1964]. (Reissue with new introduction) *Early Christian Rhetoric: The Language of the Gospel.* Cambridge, MA: Harvard University Press, 1971.

1972a   *Grace Confounding: Poems.* Philadelphia: Fortress Press.

1972b   "Vestigial Moralities in *The Sound and the Fury.*" Pp. 91–106 in *Religious Perspectives in Faulkner's Fiction.* Ed. J. R. Barth. Notre Dame, IN: Notre Dame Press.

1973–74 "Theology and Theopoetic [I]; II: The Renewal of the Religious Imagination; III: Ecstasy, Imagination and Insight." *ChCent* 90: 593–96, 1195–98; 91: 284–88.

1974a   "Reflections on Middle America." *ChCrisis* 34: 104–7.

1974b   "The Parable of the Sower: Naiveté and Method in Interpretation." *Semeia* 2: 134–51.

1975a   "Between Reminiscence and History: A Miscellany." *Proceedings of the Massachusetts Historical Society* 87: 105–17.

1975b   "Mr. W. H. Auden: Towards a New Christian Synthesis." Pp. 303–9 in *Religion and Modern Literature.* Eds. G. Tennyson and E. Ericson. Grand Rapids, MI: Eerdmans.

1975c   "In Memoriam Henry Joel Cadbury." *NTS* 21: 313–17.

1976   *Theopoetic: Theology and the Religious Imagination.* Phila-
             delphia: Fortress Press.

1977   "Revolutionary and Proletarian Poetry." Pp. 123–35 in
             Kenneth Patchen: A Collection of Essays. Ed. Richard G.
             Morgan. New York: AMS Press.

1978a   *Eschatology and Ethics in the Teaching of Jesus.* New
             York: Harper, 1939. Revised edition, 1950. (Reprinted)
             Westport, CT: Greenwood Press, 1978.

1978b   *Imagining the Real.* St. Petersburg, FL: Possum Press.
             ["Wilderiana: Dates and Places," see pp. 53–56, and
             also pp. 10–13].

1980   "New Testament Studies, 1929–1950: Reminiscences of
             a Changing Discipline." *JR* (in press).